# THE ENCHANTED DIARY

## A Teen's Guide to
## Magick and Life

# JAMIE WOOD

CELESTIAL ARTS
Berkeley | Toronto

Celestial Arts
Box 7123
Berkeley, California 94707
www.tenspeed.com

Distributed in Australia by Simon and Schuster Australia, in Canada by Ten Speed
Press Canada, in New Zealand by Southern Publishers Group, in South Africa by
Real Books, and in the United Kingdom and Europe by Airlift Book Company.

Cover and text design by Jeff Puda

Library of Congress Cataloging-in-Publication Data

Wood, Jamie.
        The enchanted diary / Jamie Wood.
            p. cm.
        ISBN-10 1-58761-245-3
        ISBN-13 978-1-58761-245-3
            1. Magic—Juvenile literature. 2. Witchcraft—Juvenile literature. I. Title

        BF1611.W848 2005
        133.4'3—dc22

                                                                2005048473

Printed in the United States of America
First printing, 2005

1 2 3 4 5 6 7 8 9 10 — 08 07 06 05

## THE ENCHANTED DIARY

Megan

I was blessed to have you have my sister and honored to have you as my friend

Love you,

Jamie Ward

# CONTENTS

# Goddess Herstory

# Rituals and Spells

# Potions Lesson

# Our Stories

# Index   190

# Acknowledgments

I have had several midwives who with their kindness and inspiration helped me birth this book. They are invaluable as resources, wise women, and great friends. Thank you to my new wonderful editor Carrie Rodrigues. I love your enthusiasm. Much love and appreciation to my literary angel, Julie Castiglia. Thanks for watching my back. And thanks to Lisa Regul, a real gem who listens to all my crazy publicity ideas. Thank you to Dennis Hayes (more a sageman than a wisewoman) whose infectious laughter and encouragement are truly appreciated. And my gratitude extends to Phil Wood and Jo Ann Deck who continue to support my books and to Kirsty Melville for getting the ball rolling. Thank you also to Jeff Puda for his awesome design. My unending gratitude goes out to Cheryl Hardin for her wisdom on the tarot, her shoulder to cry on, and pushing me when I was stubborn beyond reason. I would like to thank Deborah Halvorson for her essential oil information, mastery of herbal remedies, many of which are in the book, and companionship through creating potions, classes, and trying to stay afloat in a sea of kids. Connie DeMasters, my dear friend in Spirit, I will be forever grateful for your guidance, the confidence you gave me, and the stories you told. Mil gracias to Ms. Stella "Loopy" Luna, mi commadre and Latin mama, who donated the bath ritual. For her unconditional way of seeing me as light, I say so many thank yous to Victoria Bearden for that and her astrological help. I'm so thankful to Terin for the mask-making ritual in my last minute frenzy, Kelle for your sage advice on mentors, Waldorf graduating class of 2004, and Lisa, their amazing writing teacher, Shevaun, Delcey, Cambria, Katherine, Lisa, Chad, Suzanne, Kei, and Alana, for letting me share about writing and Wicca and your excellent essays, Lilla for teaching me belly dancing and offering your insight into the Divine Feminine, Dana Dew for being my inspiration on welcoming bliss, and to Ali for your input on the flower faeries. Lunaea Weatherstone and the Sisterhood of Willow's Magic you should know that I am so much stronger and brighter because of your support and wisdom. Mary, you reintroduced me to myself in a way that has been truly miraculous, angelic, and inspirational. I love and thank my family: Kevin, Skyler, and Kobe, my boys, for always being there for me.

Thanks to Mom! (Finally, huh?)

# Phoenix Rising

The last of her ego had gone out
In a spectacular fire of dancing flames
Grey smoke emitted from a large,
Smoldering pile of black ash

In the silence she did not mind
Her nonexistence
It was comforting to be still
Like mist rising off a quiet morning lake
Her exhalation sent another swirling of smoke
Into the bright blue sky

She watched fascinated
As the smoke took form
The ashen pile rustled and shifted
She became aware of herself
It was a strange comforting feeling
In a body no longer weighed down by pain and fear

Wings quivered on her back
Nodding and shifting her head from side to side
She blinked with child-like amazement
at the crystal sun-washed day
Was the sky always this blue?
She pushed against the ashen waste
Rising above the ground

In an instant she saw others bound to the earth
Unwilling to release their own fears
Saddened she froze

A bird sang out
Sunlight shone clear
A rainbow from a drop of dew
On a spider's web
The rain is over
"It is not your fate to be small
Nor do you serve or honor others by doing so,"
Whispered the voice of Spirit.

She closed her eyes
Her heart spoke the truth
Pumping her powerful wings
She pushed skyward
Like a bird she flew

The Phoenix reborn
Honoring my joy honors me
Honoring my truth honors Spirit
Honoring my joy honors me
Honoring my truth honors Spirit

Dancing Butterfly Who Soars on the Wind

# INTRODUCTION

*M*agick happens every day in seemingly trivial yet totally unexpected ways and in serendipitous coincidences that give you goose bumps. A miracle is always heading in your direction. Miracles and magick are yours for the asking and as natural as a blade of grass. When your emotions evolve from anger to acceptance, that's magick. When you feel the connection between a ladybug and yourself, that's magick. You are the magic!

Come on an adventure with me to deepen your understanding of how magick works in your life. Discover new ways to access your power and potential. Use the power of magick and a little self-exploration in this *Enchanted Diary* to create a world beyond your wildest dreams.

Magick is based on choice and free will. True magickal spirituality, whether you call it paganism, Wicca, Witchcraft, or something else, is imbued with creativity and matches your individual needs and desires. There are rules to follow: Harm None, do nothing against another's free will, and the Threefold Law (by which whatever you do comes back to you threefold). While these laws must be respected, the way you create magick is up to you. Your magickal path can be filled with faeries and the elemental or spiritual beings of the natural world, with a Greek or Egyptian pantheon, or with spells, or it may simply be a celebration of the cycles of the moon or seasonal holidays. Any way you mix it up is fine.

There are three types of magick: ritual magick, everyday magick, and wild magick. All three create a beautiful and enchanted life. All three require attention and following your intuition. Weaving the three together is the goal of the magick practitioner. It's also the way to uncover the Goddess within.

Ritual magick begins with focused commitment and energy, usually directed toward a specific holiday, moon phase, or intent. Through ritual magick, you set aside a special time and use concentration to cast spells or celebrate and honor changes in the planets and the seasons. Within ceremony you open up to a state of mind where all dreams are possible.

Ritual magick is ceremony and takes some form of preparation. You can make ritual magick as simple or elaborate as you like. When ritual magick is highly formalized, there are usually eleven steps to the ceremony. They consist of welcoming the participants; centering; grounding and raising the cone of power; casting or drawing a circle of protection; calling in the quarters, directions, guides, and guardians; welcoming the God and Goddess; the actual spellwork or spellcasting; enjoying cakes and ale (or juice); lowering the cone of power; thanking and bidding farewell to the directions and Deities; and erasing the circle; and closing. Suggestions on how to create these eleven stages are found in the Rituals and Spells section (page 121).

Even though there are various guidelines for setting up a sacred space for ritual magick, always do what feels right for you. Never conduct magick by rote, as if you were sleepwalking. Make sure each aspect of ritual magick means something to you. Magick moves in a circular fashion and needs room to breathe to create different possibilities.

Everyday magick occurs when you realize that each moment has the potential for miracles. Living a life filled with magick means you look for the connections between yourself and others. Pay attention to the details and moments of your life, regardless of whether they appear ordinary or extraordinary. Every moment has a little of each. When a cool breeze smelling of roses caresses your check at the exact moment you're crying because your grandmother died, and you notice it, that is everyday magick. When you're cooking or watering plants and you do it with a loving intent, you can create magick. The food will taste better and the flowers will grow taller and brighter with the attention and focus you give them. You will see that serendipity and coincidences are natural miracles.

As you listen and follow your intuition, you will be guided toward a magickal path filled with miracles. These miracles are the result of a Universal Intelligence or the Goddess or God at work in your life. Everyday magick sparkles because you see the light in every person and thing. The powerful law of attraction is another essential aspect to inviting everyday magick into your life. The more you hang out with like-minded people, the more you will draw people of your same wavelength to you. The more you focus on the positive, the more good things will happen to you. This is also true of negativity, for example, gossiping:

the more you rant on about how someone is selfish, the more you will draw selfish people to you, and draw out selfish behavior in yourself. You can draw more magick into your life by creating potions for everyday life (page 157) or by setting an intention of looking for signs from Spirit by using symbols (page 18) or the tarot (page 36). When we pay attention, we can hear answers to our questions everywhere—in snatches of conversations, song lyrics, newspaper headlines, wherever.

Wild magick is spontaneous. You can't conjure it just by willing it so. You could be hiking through the woods, swimming, or just laying out under the sun when suddenly you feel an awareness of yourself as small and yet an essential part of nature. The lines that define your physical body and the world become permeable and hazy. You are the eyes and ears of the Universe and your body is the whole world—like a drop of water that contains the whole ocean in its makeup. The whole ocean lives in you and you understand and know this is true. Then you move your body or somehow leave the meditative state and you are once again the drop of water and your own unique expression. But you are left with the understanding that absolutely everything is connected. And yet, if you tried to duplicate the exact same details, you would never be able to repeat that initial feeling. Like a breathtaking first kiss, wild magick is best when spontaneous.

Wild magick occurs most effortlessly when you are in touch with the powers of nature or the consciousness of an area or people. Practice by watching clouds and trying to imagine you are the intelligence or force that moves them. Really dive into their essence. See what happens. The section Universal Influences

THE ENCHANTED DIARY

(page 75) will give you ideas for how to connect with the Earth and with the collective consciousness—the overriding awareness or belief systems of the earth's people.

Wild magick is the manifestation and awareness of elemental energies at play. Everyone has an aspect of nature where wild magick occurs more readily for them. For some it's the beach; others feel more at home in the desert, woods, mountains, plains, valleys, rivers, or lakes, or under cloudy or wide blue skies. Can you imagine how crowded the beaches would be if everyone in the world only got their chi—their personal power or life force—from the vastness of the ocean?

Don't try to change or force yourself to feel your connection with wild magick in a certain place or in response to a certain element. Your love of a particular part of nature may change. If you live in a place that doesn't feed your soul, create pictures or paste images of your favorite part of nature into this book. In the meantime, learn to appreciate and bloom where you are planted. No flower in Spirit's garden is ever misplaced—therefore, neither can you be in the wrong place.

As a small child, perhaps before memories or logic entered, you understood the language of birds and the wind. The more you can open to nature, the better you will be able to see and feel the spirit beings in the four elements: faeries roaming the earth, sylphs flying through the air, salamanders playing in fire, and undines swimming through water. Set your intention to find, meet, and make friends with the elementals. Their energy can be a bit impish and unpredictable, or it can be serious and intense. It all depends on how you want or need to experience their energy. In other words, do you want to feel wild and wacky with your elemental playmates? Or do you prefer to connect with their sweetness? Or something in between?

The point of wild magick is to remind you of who you truly are. The trick is to bring this wild magick into everyday life and merge all that understanding into a single laser beam of energy in ritual magick that create your desires. Magick is the practice of aligning your will, or good intention, with the intelligence of the Universe. Magick helps you create a life of your choosing.

The key to being a good magician is knowing how to focus and where to put your energy. Where do your place your intent? What do you focus on exactly? There is no clear-cut answer. How, what, and where to place that energy is a unique experience to each person and constantly changes. This is why getting to know yourself and listening to your intuition is so essential to being a good and effective magician. You need to know what avenues of energy, whether playing soccer, dancing to Latin music, or painting, help you clear your mind long enough to hear your heart.

This *Enchanted Diary* is a journey into you. What an adventure! Diaries are some of the greatest, most valuable books you will ever read or own. They help you build a foundation for self-trust and support you in becoming your own best friend. They rarely talk back (and if they do, you can just slam the book shut!). They listen to all your whining, ranting, dreaming, wishing, and creating, and they never go away.

You will never reach a magic age when the entire world makes sense, when you know it all, or even when you become comfortable with not having all the answers. But using a diary helps you understand who you are, where you hope to go, and possible ways to get there. Through self-knowledge, you will naturally discover your ability to create a life of your choosing. So even if you're not

THE ENCHANTED DIARY

sure how it will all unfold, being in touch with how you operate and what you want makes the road of life much easier.

A diary is a roadmap to the hidden you. With self-knowledge, you can access the tools and talents you need to bring your unique gifts into the world. You can chip away the excess, getting to the core of your light and beauty. Knowing and accepting yourself helps you be strong even when friendships go awry, when a boy you like asks another girl to the winter formal, when rumors circulate about you like the Energizer Bunny, or when your mom yells at you in front of your friends.

Record what you feel, not how you think you should feel, or how your best friend, big sister, or mother or father would prefer you to feel. In a diary, you get to be accepted just as you are. And even if someone reads this diary who shouldn't, what they will find is you on a path of power. No one can take that away from you. Each and every step you make along the way is embedded into your mind, body, and soul. It's yours forever.

Used in retrospect, diaries provide a window to the past, an opportunity to see when or how you built patterns of self-confidence, self-worth, or joy, or, on the other hand, shame, anger, or pain. If the pattern is positive, looking back at the incidents that created those feelings can help deepen or reinforce your confidence. If the pattern is destructive, looking at the original event after some time has passed helps you see the poison for what it is. With a different perspective, you can begin to recognize more than just the pain and perhaps find the silver lining. Your perspective is a choice you make.

You choose how you are going to interact with or react to every person, place, or thing in your life. Acknowledging your power to choose widens the horizon of possible reactions and creates more space for positive solutions. I'm not saying you can be perfect or ignore your feelings in an attempt to see the silver lining all the time—just remember that it's there when you are ready.

Take these pages and learn to develop your intuition, power, self-reliance, and trust in yourself. Allow your innate ability to manifest magick to blossom and grow. You don't have to go through this book from front to back. You can open up and dig in wherever you find yourself. Allowing Spirit to guide you is often the best way to get started in magick, journaling, or creating. You don't even have to write—use whatever ever form of creativity or expression calls to you. And enjoy!

# INNER GIRL

*I*t is important to discover the truth about yourself before you can put your power into action. You must uncover your patterns of behavior, know your talents and limitations, and then wisely and slowly challenge your actions, talents, and limits.

Getting to know yourself takes a long time, in part because we often lie to ourselves about what we can or can't do and in part because what we consider important in life constantly changes. However, learning who and what you are today is essential to developing your power. Your expression, personality, and spirit are so unique and needed in the world that without them the world is less beautiful. I promise you that this is true. Once you become aware of your inclinations and what you do unconsciously as a reflex action, and you will discover how to direct magick into your life.

Throughout this chapter, there are several quizzes and other tools to help you uncover and confirm truths about you and how you operate. Many of the quizzes are designed with preset answers and conclusions. If you're inspired or if you despise labels, feel free to come up with another answer, write an essay in response, or even create a whole new conclusion to the question. Just like a spell or a recipe, these quizzes are created to get you thinking and feeling about an issue, not to give you a set answer that can't evolve to accommodate your individuality.

Sometimes you will feel comfortable with more than one answer, and that's perfectly okay. Think about it: you have are more than one personality—you're one person when out to dinner with your parents, but another side of you shows up when you're giggling your fool head off at the movies with friends. And it's not being fake to alter who you are: it's human nature, and sometimes a matter of survival. The point of the quizzes in this chapter is to recognize your tendencies so you can be proactive rather than reactive. In other words, pinpointing how you are most inclined to act can help you respond how you want to, not overreact and experience a flood of regret later. In between each breath, each wave on the ocean, there is a pause, however slight. In that pause we make a choice among all the possibilities in a given situation.

The quizzes will help you know more about yourself and strengthen your resolve within that pause, and give you a better opportunity to see the different choices and choose wisely. Get a better understanding of your foundation and personality with the elementals quiz. The clairs quiz helps develop your intuition. Working with symbols enables you to see where your thinking has become rigid and frees you to open up. Use the flower faeries quiz to get in touch with nature. The tarot information gives you a guide for navigating your life, and palmistry can tell you a bit how you see your life today and how you can move forward. Use Athena's Animals to gain insight about your inner Goddess. And you can transform nightmares into powerful guardians with the shape-shifting quiz.

Sometimes these tests will hit the nail on the head. You may feel completely vulnerable because a stranger (that's me) described you perfectly. But it's all good. After you get over the shock, it feels good to be seen, don't ya think? Knowing who you are gives you better tools to navigate life. Plus it's fun! So jump in.

# Elementals

The elements of nature—air, fire, water, and earth—are the building blocks for life and creating magick. Everyone tends to rely on one of the four elements over the others. The pentacle, a symbol of the Craft, is a five-pointed star inside a circle. The points of the star represent air, fire, water, earth, and Spirit. The circle represents the unending circle of life, within which the elements and Spirit are interconnected, working together harmoniously. The pentacle is also the symbol created if you were to stand with arms and legs outstretched within a circle. The pentacle represents nature and our connection to it.

The key to directing magick is moderation and balance of energy. Just as the pentacle is equally divided, like the spokes of a wheel, it is important to understand and balance the power of each element. You are the channel or vessel through which miracles and magick happen. You need to figure out where you often place your energy so you can learn how to best call on it when you need it and which elements you need to focus on to create balance. Learning which element you rely upon and what that means can help you when you feel out of sorts. Taking a bath does wonders for a water baby, while gardening or digging your toes into mud really helps an earth mama.

Let me give you an example of how knowing which element dominates your personality can affect you. I am an earth sign—very much so. Recently my family journeyed to New Orleans. I didn't realize how much I'd be impacted by this city being eight to eleven feet below sea level. Also, the city is very old, with loads of magick and ghosts and a powerful magickal community and it became a swirling mass of images for me. I felt as though I had entered a dream where everything I knew and understood had turned upside down. It was like Alice in Wonderland meets Mr. Toad's Wild Ride. I felt fearful and panic-stricken, not excited.

I couldn't ground myself or feel centered in my normal way. I couldn't get a grip as if I was free-falling turning backward somersaults.

After freaking out for a couple of hours, I called an earthy High Priestess and asked for support. She reminded me that I wasn't going to be able to dig my toes into mud in the way I wanted, and said I'd better let go of my unyielding ways and get used to the floating. Once I did, I had a much better time swimming than trying to walk underwater.

When you are scared or out of your comfort zone, you may attack aspects of yourself or project the reason for your fear onto others. It is important not to strike out and divide yourself against

THE ENCHANTED DIARY

your allies, but to unite instead. Do not wait for some magick to save you like a faery tale. Become aware of your surroundings and gather power from the elements around you. You can do it!

Now try the quiz and see whether you resonate with air, fire, water, or earth.

**Read each pair of statements and choose the one that describes you best:**

*1.* **A** – I rely upon fate and imagination to get out of trouble.
   **B** – I worry about how things will turn out.

*2.* **A** – I like to be on the stage and have an audience.
   **B** – I prefer to direct the performers.

*3.* **A** – My wardrobe has a colorful, trendy flair.
   **B** – My style is classic, high-quality, and timeless.

*4.* **A** – My dreams are more important than my goals.
   **B** – My goals are more important than my dreams.

*5.* **A** – I'm always in trouble, but it's so much fun.
   **B** – I don't feel comfortable rocking the boat.

*6.* **C** – I speak my truth despite the consequence.
   **D** – I tailor my words to make sure I don't offend others.

7. **C** – I make quick, impulsive decisions.

   **D** – I prefer slow-moving, subtle changes.

8. **C** – I am possessive with friends and people I love.

   **D** – I give my friends and people I love room to grow.

9. **C** – I dream of traveling to exotic places and trying weird foods.

   **D** – I like to snuggle with loved ones beside a roaring fire.

10. **C** – I have good ideas but prefer to let someone else do the work.

    **D** – I find great accomplishment in seeing a project to its end.

Add up how many As, Bs, Cs, and Ds you picked.

The two most common letters in your results will reveal where your powers lie.

| **A** and **C** | **A** and **D** | **B** and **C** |
|---|---|---|
| **B** and **D** | | |
| Fire | Water | Air | Earth |

THE ENCHANTED DIARY

# FIRE

You are a spark plug, honey. You are passionate, daring, and expressive. Once you get going, it's hard to stop you. You have lots of courage and a strong will. You jump into action and usually hit the ground running. Fire gives you a knack for transforming or changing situations with charm or force—either one works for you. You bring healing and introduce knowledge with your enthusiasm. Be careful not to burn bridges with your fire and do remember that stability doesn't have to mean boring. Your magickal creature is a dragon and your magickal tool is a sword.

# AIR

You are a beacon of light and playfulness. You are intelligent, impulsive, curious, artsy, and flexible. Often inspired by fresh ideas and new ways of doing things, you use your intellect and logic to solve problems. Independence, freedom, and fairness are very important to you. You enjoy playing with the wind and don't mind changes. Others are attracted to your light, wit, charm, and friendliness. Dreams of flying and moving at fast speeds are your favorites. Allow your heart to lead the way once in a while, exploring your sensations, not just your beautiful mind. Your magickal creature is an eagle and your magickal tool is a wand.

# WATER

You are a boundless sprite—sensitive, compassionate, imaginative, and accepting. You can adapt to almost any situation with ease. You are willing to experience the deepest, darkest places and are sometimes quite secretive. Your feelings run as deep and vast as the mysteries of the world, which intrigue you. Your intuition is strong, you are psychically in tune, and you sense things others are unaware of. You can be sensual, romantic, caring, and in love with love. Take care not to get too inwardly focused, personalizing everything, and remember that everyone is the star of her own drama. Your magickal animal is a dolphin and your magickal tool is a cup or chalice.

## EARTH

Earth mamas sizzle with raw physical energy. You have the persistence and ability to manifest your dreams and climb the highest mountains. You are driven, loyal, practical, and strong. Your ability to nurture is valued more than you realize. You know how to be silent and wait. You may get frustrated, but you have tremendous endurance and rarely give up. Integrity and honesty in others impresses you. You have an earthy, organic style. Every once in a while, lift your roots out of the ground and do something utterly silly and without purpose. Your magickal creature is a stag and your magickal tool is a pentacle.

Once we recognize our tendencies, we can focus our energy in the direction we prefer rather than be used by the energy without a bearing. And though we all generally tend to use one element more than the others, these elements are, of course, a generalization. The entire population of the world can't neatly fit into just four categories. You may even feel drawn to two elements. And yes, the element you identify with often corresponds with your astrological, or Sun Sign. Aquarius, Gemini, and Libra are air signs. Aries, Leo, and Sagittarius are fire signs. Pisces, Cancer, and Scorpio are water signs. Taurus, Virgo, and Capricorn are earth signs. Check out the astrological information on page 25. Record any thoughts about what you learned here.

_____

_____

_____

_____

_____

_____

_____

_____

_____

_____

_____

_____

_____

_____

_____

_____

_____

_____

_____

_____

_____

_____

Take each element in turn and meditate with a representation of that energy—air, fire, water, or earth. By meditation I mean just "be" with the element. For example, sit outside and watch the wind blow the trees, or sit in front of a candle flame or a bowl of water, or sit on the ground and sift your fingers through dirt. You can also try to invoke the elements by facing the direction each corresponds with: air is east, fire is south, water is west, and earth is north. Call out for the element. Ask the beings that live in each element to visit you. In the sylphs fly through the air; salamanders live and play in fire; undines and water sprites swim in water; and gnomes and faeries roam the earth. Move your body to represent the elements and play with the energies. Remember, witches and Wiccans pagans, or Goddess and nature lovers actually *practice* magick—they don't perform or perfect it. This is practice. Allow for learning curves.

Now write down what you learned from the quiz and meditation. Listen for any advice the element would like to give you. Be sure not to combine two elements in the same sitting. Allow each to have its own space with you.

# The Clairs

Everyone is psychic. Everyone has the innate ability to tap into and improve her inner resources and connection to the Divine inside and the Creative Source. Psychic messages, feelings, and intuition can be defined as a direct knowing of something without conscious use of reason. That gut feeling or inner voice is familiar to all of us, but knowing where those feelings and voices originate takes some skill and experience. Take this quiz to find out which of the ways of understanding "clear knowledge" you have: clairaudience, clairvoyance, clairsentience, or clairessence.

*1.* **When you can't decide on something, you**
- **A** – Go somewhere silent and be still
- **B** – Look around for something to catch your attention and help you out
- **C** – Go about your business waiting for an answer to come
- **D** – Go out in nature or curl up with something favorite and comfortable

*2.* **When you're studying for a test, you first**
- **A** – Hum, play music, or put on the TV and repeat the information aloud
- **B** – Use color-coded highlighters, tabs, or flash cards
- **C** – Delve into notes and reread the book
- **D** – Breathe deeply and pay close attention to your surroundings

**3.** **You are most turned on when**

    **A** – Your crush says something sweet and endearing

    **B** – Your crush dresses fine and compliments how you look

    **C** – Your crush remembers something you told him or her that was important to you

    **D** – Your crush feels familiar, like you've known him or her forever

**4.** **Your favorite book is the best because**

    **A** – You know exactly what the main character sounds like

    **B** – You can imagine and see the events as they happen

    **C** – You feel the emotions of the main characters

    **D** – You can smell the salt in the ocean or the apple pie baking in the oven

**5.** **You approach an authority (parent, teacher, boss) on difficult issues by**

    **A** – Sticking to the parts of the topic you can talk about with sincerity

    **B** – Logically explaining the situation as you see it

    **C** – Taking a deep breath and plunging ahead

    **D** – Moving with caution, keenly picking up on changes in the other's mood

6. **If you're upset, you prefer a friend to**
    **A** – Tell you everything is going to be alright
    **B** – Give you a big hug and say nothing
    **C** – Tell you that no matter what happens you'll be okay
    **D** – Make or bring you your favorite food

7. **When you're doing something you shouldn't be**
    **A** – Your four other senses dull, but your ears perk up
    **B** – Your keen eyes narrow, observe, and assess the situation
    **C** – You notice or feel trouble from your gut
    **D** – You detect trouble in the air

If you chose mostly As, you have clairaudience. If you chose mostly Bs, you're clairvoyant. If you chose mostly Cs, you're clairsentient. If you chose mostly Ds, you have clairessence.

# CLAIRAUDIO

*Clairaudio* means "clear hearing." You hear the voice of wisdom inside and often hear things others don't. This might be mysterious voices, especially right after a loved one has crossed over or died, or you may clearly hear someone speaking in your dreams or her music seemingly from nowhere. The way to improve your gift is to be sensitive to your talent and surround yourself with pleasing noises. Avoid loud people and places. Imagine the sweetness of this: if you placed a constellation on a musical scale, the stars would play the most etheric, angelic music. Find whatever sounds lift you up to a place where you feel connected to all that is. Record what you hear in either words or symbols and bless it with your belief in its authenticity.

## CLAIRVOYANT

*Clairvoyant* means "clear seeing." You see situations from the highest point of truth. Sometimes you can even see events in the future. Who needs a crystal ball when you have a vision of an accident or of meeting a friend before it happens? You are particularly sensitive to light and visual beauty. Here's how you can improve your talent: Before you get out of bed in the morning, imagine a purple light shining just behind your third eye, which is located between your eyebrows and just a bit higher up. Rub this spot in a clockwise manner, and think of it as cleaning a window. Believe you see clearly that which cannot be defined in logical terms and follow the advice you are given by your gift of clairvoyance. Write down what you see and track how it compares to reality if and when it does happen.

## CLAIRSENTIENT

*Clairsentient* means "clear feeling." You intuitively sense the feelings of people and just know or feel things in ways that often cannot be explained. People who fall into this category are called "empaths" and make great healers. Like a veritable sponge, you take in the emotions of others. While this can be a wonderful gift it can also be a most difficult path if you don't learn when you can help and when you need to allow others the dignity of getting themselves out of hot water. To improve the gift of clear feeling, hold your arms out so you form a T shape. Imagine you are gathering the ends of your aura: Make a fist and quickly pull your hands to your sides. Repeat this two more times. This brings your aura in closer so that you don't take on more than you should. Now imagine a light growing in your solar plexus, just above your belly button. See the light fill your entire body. Write about times when you followed the messages from your clairsentience or intuition.

## CLAIRESSENCE

*Clairessence* means "clear essence." You have the ability to intuitively smell or detect the flavor, fragrance, or essence of people, places, and things. For example, the scent of roses often wafts through the air when a great healing has occurred or when a person who has crossed over comes to pay a visit; you will be the first to sense it. Our sense of smell originates in the oldest part of our brain and is closely linked to memories. So you will be comforted by things that are familiar or that you connect with happy, carefree times. Avoid synthetic oils and perfumes, factories, and toxic fumes (that's a good one for all of us to avoid!). You are particularly sensitive to aromatherapy and can truly benefit from its many advantages. Play with essential oils to fine-tune your gift. Try using the oils to alter your mood the next time you feel angry or sad. Discover which oils you really like. Make the Perfectly You Perfume (page 162) and write about how you feel when you wear the perfume.

Most everyone has one intuitive ability that outshines the others, and some people have the ability to tap into a few. Intuition is like a muscle: it must be worked on a regular basis to grow and improve, so practice working with your talent. Don't let others' ignorance or fear stand between you and your power. The world needs strong intuitive women. Write about your experiences with practicing your intuition.

---------------------------------------------------------------

---------------------------------------------------------------

---------------------------------------------------------------

---------------------------------------------------------------

---------------------------------------------------------------

---------------------------------------------------------------

---------------------------------------------------------------

---------------------------------------------------------------

---------------------------------------------------------------

---------------------------------------------------------------

---------------------------------------------------------------

---------------------------------------------------------------

---------------------------------------------------------------

---------------------------------------------------------------

---------------------------------------------------------------

---------------------------------------------------------------

---------------------------------------------------------------

---------------------------------------------------------------

---------------------------------------------------------------

---------------------------------------------------------------

---------------------------------------------------------------

# Symbols

Symbols allow you to see through your mind's eye, trust your gut's intuition, and bypass your logical mind, which can get caught up in what the eye sees. Symbols represent a vast world of feelings and sensations that are difficult to describe with words, which box in their boundless spirit. Think about how, when you study for an exam, just one person, say Hitler, can represent a flood of emotions and facts.

Images affect us on a conscious and an unconscious level. For example, you could just hate whales regardless of the fact that they are loving, gentle creatures and every animal totem book tells you whales are the keepers of the earth records (what has happened since the beginning of time). It doesn't matter—you just don't like them. However, with the brainstorming technique I describe on page 28, you may discover or remember that you once went on a whale-watching trip and puked your guts out in front of all your friends. Then you projected your embarrassment onto the whales and now despise them.

With awareness of what these symbols mean to you, you can begin to understand yourself better, and understanding usually opens the door to acceptance. With acceptance you can begin to deepen your talents, being in full awareness of your gifts and limitations and honoring them both. Then, when symbols appear in your life, you can begin to broaden the ways you look at them. From that vantage point, you can see if you agree with all the associations you've made, or if some have begun to get a little worn-out and no longer serve your highest good: Do you feel good when you think that way? Are you honoring your true self and needs?

 **Ankh**
life, regeneration, everlasting life

**Cauldron**
womb, the void before creation, water, feminine energy

**Cross**
(Christian or Latin) resurrection, hope, sacrifice

**Cross**
(Equal or Solar) balance, the movement of the sun

**Cup/Chalice**
womb, the void before creation, water, feminine energy

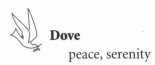
**Dove**
    peace, serenity

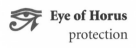
**Eye of Horus**
    protection

**Fish**
    Brotherhood and faith

**God**
    male energy of the seed of life, action

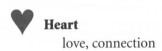
**Goddess/Triple Moon Maiden**
    Mother, and Crone as the waxing, full,
    and waning moon; feminine energy, mystery,
    and psychic abilities

**Heart**
    love, connection

    THE ENCHANTED DIARY

**∞ Infinity**
the connection and constant motion of all life

**♂ Mars**
male, aggression, combativeness

**☽ Moon**
female energy, rest, rejuvenation, mystery

 **Omkar**
om, the primordial sound, the beginning,
awareness

**☮ Peace**
peace, harmony

**⛤ Pentacle**
Witchcraft, the four elements or directions
connected to Spirit and surrounded by the
circle of life

**Septagram/Faery Star/Elvin Star**
spirituality, the faery and elvin realm, play

**Spiral Goddess**
evolution, rebirth, counter-clockwise, rest

**Spiral**
spirituality, growth, clockwise, action

**Sun**
male energy, action, growth

**Triangle**
(Air) intuition, intelligence, beginnings,
the element of the east

**Triangle**
(Earth) ancestry, stability, grounding,
the element of the north

△ **Triangle**
   (Fire) ascension, growth, transformation,
   the element of the south

▽ **Triangle**
   (Water) vagina or womb, nature, creation,
   the element of the west

 **Triquetra**
   Celtic symbol of the Triple Goddess (Maiden,
   Mother, Crone), the three elements of nature
   (land, sky, sea)

 **Triskele/Triple Spiral/Triskelion**
   Celtic symbol of the power of life and rebirth,
   Triple Goddess, manifestation

♀ **Venus**
   female energy, love, kindness

**Wheel**
(of the Year) eight sabbats or holy days in the ever-changing year, continuity

 **Yin Yang**
balance in opposites, especially male and female or light and dark energy

## NUMBERS

*1* – centeredness, creativity, protection, kindness

*2* – duality, imagination, dreaming, sensitivity, conception

*3* – manifestation, expansion, education, travel

*4* – balance, individuality, originality, tolerance

*5* – teaching, communication, flexibility, movement

*6* – love, nurturing, compassion, romance

*7* – spirituality, mystery, sensitivity, faith

*8* – infinity, wisdom, patience, stability

*9* – endings, courage, conflict, initiative

*10* – beginnings, love and light, manifestation

# ASTROLOGICAL OR ZODIAC SIGNS

The dates of the astrological signs actually vary from year to year. Aries could begin on the 20th one year and on the 21st another year. If you were born between the 19th and the 23rd of any month, you are considered to be on the cusp, although you will have a dominant sign.

♈ **Aries**
*(March 20/22–April 20/22)*
warrior spirit, daredevil, courageous, survivor

♉ **Taurus**
*(April 20/22–May 20/22)*
silent, steadfast, pleasure seeking, strong

♊ **Gemini**
*(May 20/22–June 20/22)*
teacher, imaginative, curious, adaptable

♋ **Cancer**
*(June 20/22–July 20/22)*
healer/mother, feeling, accepting, nurturing

## Leo
*(July 20/22–August 20/22)*
performer, charming, celebratory, dynamic

## Virgo
*(August 20/22–September 20/22)*
seeker, perfectionist, unassuming, helpful

## Libra
*(September 20/22–October 20/22)*
peacemaker, easygoing, indecisive, changeable

## Scorpio
*(October 20/22–November 20/22)*
mysterious, passionate, cool and collected, gentle

## Sagittarius
*(November 20/22–December 20/22)*
gypsy, hopeful, adventurous, open

## Capricorn
*(December 20/22–January 20/22)*
climber, driven, practical, integrity

## Aquarius
*(January 20/22–February 20/22)*
freedom fighter, independent, rebellious, honest

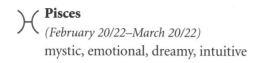

**Pisces**
*(February 20/22–March 20/22)*
mystic, emotional, dreamy, intuitive

# COLORS

**Blue** – calm, healing, centeredness, water, communication, possibilities, truth

**Green** – healing, nature, growth, renewal, earth

**Yellow** – courage, hope, sunshine, danger, will, joy

**Orange** – exciting, spirituality, creativity, openness, enthusiasm

**Red** – grounding, anger, action, fire, security

**Purple** – spirituality, royalty, Divine protection, true seeing, intuition

**Pink** – friendship, love, forgiveness, devotion

**Black** – the unknown, mystery, protection, independence

**White** – truth, purity, wisdom, understanding

**Brown** – grounding, earth, dependability, considerateness, order

**Gray** – fear, dignity, self-control, responsibility, dullness

Take a symbol from the previous list or any symbol that intrigues you. This can be a symbol you receive while dreaming or day-dreaming. Draw lines from the symbol outward and write its meaning to you. See how many different ways you can describe what the symbol means to you. For example, if you drew a picture of a wave, perhaps connecting ideas or images could be a dolphin, floating diamonds sparkling on the water, seaweed, or vacations. The important thing is that you connect with the image in as many ways as possible. Even though I included meanings for the symbols, I encourage you to create your own meanings and significance for them. Circle the symbols that have meaning for you or inspire feeling in you, then write about how those symbols make you feel and what thoughts they inspire. Or draw other symbols and describe what they mean to you.

You give symbols their life and texture through your awareness of how they apply to you. Use the blank space that follows to explore your thoughts and feelings about a symbol or two. You will be amazed to see some of the connections that emerge that you hadn't consciously recognized. Since there may be many symbols that are meaningful to you or spark your interest, you might want to get a special notebook just for symbols so you'll have plenty of space to explore them.

THE ENCHANTED DIARY

# Flower Faeries

There was never a flower that was misplaced in the garden of heaven and earth. You, too, can never be in a wrong situation—there is always something to learn from any situation. Even if you are in an environment that seems to restrict your true colors, you can learn resiliency and figure out a way to protect your essence until you are free to shine. Take the vastness of your light and focus it like a laser beam of unique brightness.

We cannot be all the flowers at once. Each of us is a particular face or facet of the Goddess's exquisite diamond. There is no point in trying to be something you are not. Just be the best you can be and express your beauty as fully as you can. Only that way can the Goddess be there for you and be present in the world. Be the bright light, like the flower spirits, called devas. Try this quiz to help you get in touch with your flower self, your essence, and all the characteristics of your flower faery.

**A real adventure would be:**

    **A** – Rock climbing

    **B** – A silent retreat

    **C** – Camping under the stars

    **D** – A hotel without room service

**If you were a dog, which would you be:**

    **A** – Great Dane

    **B** – Greyhound

**C** – Golden retriever

**D** – Pomeranian

**If your wardrobe consisted of only two colors, which combination would they most likely be:**

**A** – Yellow and orange

**B** – Black and white

**C** – Blue and green

**D** – Red and pink

**If you were stranded on a desert island and could only have one spice, which would it be:**

**A** – Salt

**B** – Nutmeg

**C** – Cinnamon

**D** – Pepper

**The moment you leave the house you must have your:**

**A** – Purse

**B** – Unnoticeable charm, trinket, or totem

**C** – Music

**D** – Lipstick

If you chose mostly As, you are a sunflower. If you chose mostly Bs, you are a calla lily. If you chose mostly Cs, you are a daisy. If you chose mostly Ds, you are a rose. Claim this flower essence by reading the description below aloud.

## SUNFLOWER

I am a sunflower—joyous, sunny, and happy. I am open to the world and its experiences. I am ready, willing, and trusting. I want to receive all the gifts of the world, and I am excited to be part of life. I choose to get up every morning and look for that silver lining, even on the cloudiest days. I prefer the warmth of the day and follow the sun, wherever he goes. I reach for the outer limits and grow as tall and big as I can. I am slightly disappointed when the day is over. But I know how to make the best of bad, sad, or dead things. I know how to create birth from death. I have courage and can shelter others. I'm strong, capable, and a jester in hard times. I am willing and able to help others. They smile when they see me. I like that.

## CALLA LILY

I am a calla lily with an inner strength that can rarely be shaken. I don't need a lot of attention. I grow without you even noticing. Sometimes I prefer the blanket of invisibility and quiet. I am classic, graceful, and poised, and I know who I am. I unravel myself very slowly, but once I pass the crucial opening stage, I will continue to reveal my secrets. It gives me great comfort to grow alongside my sisters. And yet I can grow alone, for I am quite independent. I may not follow the most common expectations and roads, but whatever I do has an unmatched refinement and skill. I can rock your world.

## DAISY

I am a daisy and able to multiply happiness all around me. I spread joy by the mere smile on my face and twinkle in my eye.

I am encouraging and can lift others' spirits. I am playful and unconcerned with details or weighty issues. That's not to say I shy away from feelings. I can cry, and when I do, it breaks hearts. Once I've tasted my first tear or disappointment, I am forever changed and ready for more risks and unpredictable adventures in life. I want to dance and feel the wind in my hair. I am free and ready to be sensual. I will always believe that everything I do is pure. Don't ever tell me it's not, because this world needs my faith to be happy and have hope.

## ROSE

I am a rose—demanding, strong, and beautiful. I understand my worth and don't need to explain myself or make excuses. I am fragile because I need a lot of attention and praise to grow, but I know how to protect myself. Each winter that passes gives me more confidence and strength. When I am in bloom, people feel compelled to stop and comment. It angers me to be weak, and I want my own space. (Trust me I can take your trash and turn it into something beautiful.) I want each phase of my growth to be honored. I am generous and will give as much if not more than I am given. I am unafraid to tell you what I need. I am regal, powerful, loving, sometimes misunderstood, but always resilient.

On the following pages, write or draw about your flower essence or create a new flower to associate with.

THE ENCHANTED DIARY

Inner Girl

# The Tarot

The tarot is a pictographic language that helps create a bridge between your logical and symbolic mind. Through the use of pictures, colors, and symbols, the cards' images bring together the conscious and subconscious aspects of you to work in harmony. The use of symbols speaks to the part of your brain that defies logic and believes all things are possible. It awakens you to the hidden powers within.

The tarot consists of Minor and Major Arcana cards. The Minor Arcana offers guidance on everyday experiences. The Major Arcana represents archetypes that can teach you about your philosophy of life and approach to living. The archetypes symbolize different powers we all have access to. They offer a window into our beliefs, help us understand our relationships with people and life, and give us tools to discover our life's purpose.

You can determine your soul and personality cards with a little math. Your soul card represents your life lessons and the journey you have chosen for this lifetime. Your personality card symbolizes the means by which you carry out your karma. Just add together your birth year, birth month, and birth date. For example, for a person born on December 23, 1988, it would work out like this:

$$
\begin{array}{r}
1991 \\
12 \\
+ \quad 23 \\
\hline
2026 = 2 + 2 + 6 = 10
\end{array}
$$

In this case, the personality card would be 10, or the Wheel of Fortune. Keep any number between 1 and 22. Any number over 23 needs to be added together. For example, if you got 24, you would add 2 + 4 and get 6. If your number is between 1 and 10, that's both your personality and soul card. If your number is over 10, reduce it again by adding the two numbers together. Most tarot readers say the larger number is the personality card, and the smaller number is the soul card; some say the opposite. However, since the Major Arcana archetypes teach us about our soul's journey through this life, it works both ways.

Now do the same calculations for your year card. Although you can do this at any time, it would be a nice ritual to do every year on your birthday. The year card reveals which archetype will guide you through the year. It can help you figure out what the year may hold and how you will express yourself in it. Add your birthday to the current year. For example, if you're calculating your year card for the year of 2006, and your birthday is January 22, it would work out like this:

$$2006$$
$$1$$
$$+\ \ 22$$
$$\overline{\phantom{2006}}$$
$$2029 = 2 + 2 + 9 = 13$$

While the Major Arcana represents archetypes found in human nature and phases of human life, look for an aspect of their symbolism that makes sense to you. Twenty different books on the tarot will give you twenty slightly different interpretations of the cards (which is why I consulted five tarot readers for this section).

The cards symbolize general characteristics and tendencies. Your own interpretation of the symbols is the key to understanding how their messages apply in your life.

There are many ways to learn the symbols and archetypes of the Major Arcana. Here's one way: Every morning, ask your guides or Spirit how your day will be, what you need to pay attention to, or some similar question, then lay out one or three cards. Review the cards at the end of the day and see how their message played out. Another way is to take each card in turn and put it facedown under your pillow before you go to sleep at night. In the morning, record any message that came to you. Or you can allow the card's message to influence the next day and record your thoughts before you go to bed. Take a break at least one night; twenty-two archetypes in twenty-two days is a lot of information. Another way to learn about tarot is to look at the cards and write down your own interpretation of the symbols, regardless of what books may say. You need to relate the cards to your own experience so that what you learn becomes your own. When it comes to your life, *you* are the best psychic out there.

## *1*~MAGICIAN / MAGUS

The Magician is a teacher who works as a channel or instrument for bringing the wisdom, light, and love of heaven to earth. There is simplicity and a free spirit here. The Magician holds the power of will and individuality and the act of creating, and walks with awareness, constantly striving to balance between light and dark and between all opposites. Be careful to not be manipulative for your own sake, to keep your ego in check, and to always teach and guide in service to humanity. Connect to your self—think it, be it, create it.

# 2 ~ PRIESTESS

The Priestess represents the faces of the Goddess (Maiden, Enchantress Mother, and Crone). She seeks inner guidance and enlightenment from the unknown as she holds the power of still-ness. The Priestess is the guardian of mysteries, the unconscious, the void before creation, dreams, and symbols. She is everything that is divinely feminine—feelings, spiral movement, intuition. She knows the truth of our essence and is able to bring this forth into life. Remember: Even though you have wisdom to impart, there's always more to learn. Know that to trust yourself is to trust Spirit. Tune into the cosmic song.

# 3 ~ EMPRESS

The Empress represents Mother Earth energy and attracting opportunities by being receptive. She holds the Divine Feminine, maternal instinct, nurturing, life's cycles and rhythms, beauty, and compassion. She manifests through her connection to love, nature, and beauty. She is the essence of the creative force and patroness of actors, writers, poets, and all forms of creativity. The Empress brings life into every situation, has high emotional intelligence, and is pregnant with all possibilities. Be careful to not smother, be possessive, or make anyone or anything the object of your love. True love is unconditional, without strings or attachment.

# 4 ~ EMPEROR

The Emperor is the courageous, knowing, responsible conqueror and leader. Determined to achieve, he must constantly practice discernment and maintain his sensitivity to keeping the balance of opposites. He is dependent upon higher wisdom, guided by the sun, and kept to his good intentions and valor. This is the archetype of the tough but fair ruler, who represents grace under fire. He has a firm grip on reality. Don't conquer in vain or become seduced by your own power. Maintain your vulnerability and humility through all your many successes, and be sure to use your talents to serve humankind.

## *5* ~ PRIEST / HIEROPHANT

The Priest is the patient protector and caring father figure who heeds and brings the knowledge of the ancestors. A practical teacher and a shepherd of lost ones, he is able to align knowledge and reason. The Priest understands duality and can maintain the balance between polar opposites, which helps him be a good mediator. Constantly in the search for the extraordinary in the ordinary, the Priest guides with an open hand and hopeful heart. A peacemaker, trusting, trustworthy, and the keeper of faith, he knows how to bring spiritual consciousness into the mundane world. Don't become too intoxicated with your own counsel.

## *6* ~ LOVERS

Lovers see the beauty in life and in the diversity that makes life and people so wonderful. This archetype is the symbol of heaven and earth reaching out to each other until their ultimate integration. It is the place of connection where consciousness or thought and manifestation and expression meet. This symbol encourages trust in intimacy and relationships, increased self-love, and finding centeredness. The Lovers archetype helps us to see and find love that transcends conditions and rules and to make decisions based on higher truths and wisdom. It guides us toward creating a path with heart. Through the Lovers, we find harmony and commitment. Be careful not to make anyone an obsession or the object of your love, and don't get overly mesmerized by romantic love.

## 7 ~ CHARIOT

The Chariot holds the power of forward movement and the positive use of self-control. This archetype teaches balance with the wild nature of the animal within with the desires, ego, and strength of the rider until the two become one. The charioteer usually has a lot going on and focus is the name of the game. The rider gracefully and lightly guides the wildness without trying to rein it in too hard, which allows the untamable to be channeled into vast strength. The charioteer must trust intuition, treat oneself with gentleness, and allow for a learning curve. Beware of procrastination and be attentive to the methods you use to attain your goals.

## 8 ~ STRENGTH / ADJUSTMENT / LUST

The Strength archetype is the symbol of everlasting infinity, the alpha and omega, beginnings and endings. The just use of will, truth, and endurance represented in this card comes from the cosmos and cannot be deterred. This card also symbolizes the connection between beauty's refinement and the raw strength and courage of the beast. Strength has endured much and must find the courage to walk away when necessary and enjoy the bliss of the moment. Here is the champion of the underdog and a warrior whose passion is linked to Spirit. Be cautious of your hotheadedness and learn how best to channel your enthusiasm through strengthening your core essence to create and manifest.

## *9* ~ HERMIT

The Hermit has her back to the world. Unafraid of solitude, she walks the path of the Seeker. She must do what is right for herself, holding a light to show the way for others even if they don't follow. The light is the Star of David, symbolizing "As above, so below," which means the knowledge of heaven meets with the feelings of earth to bring understanding. The hermit often takes the path less traveled and is sometimes sought after for her wisdom. From time to time, she craves socialization. Isolation is necessary for her to learn to trust her self, her inner voice and light, as well as her own guidance, before she can ascend toward unconditional love and wisdom. Be careful not to become so isolated that you avoid relationships. Let your intuition guide the way.

## *10* ~ WHEEL OF FORTUNE

The Wheel of Fortune represents blessings, abundance, and the overall good within the world. Often depicted with a single eye, the Wheel of Fortune symbolizes how "good" can come from "bad" and that, with an objective perspective, all will balance out and the Universe will bring the right circumstance for your growth. Change must be embraced. The four elements are represented and the circle symbolizes the continuity of life. This card reminds us to enjoy what's going right and speaks to the freedom that comes from trusting in Spirit. This is an evolutionary lifetime and the opportunity to move to a higher vibration. It is time to fulfill your dharma (your soul's mission) and karma (balancing debts from this and past lives). Don't become paralyzed by overanalyzing, and don't wait for others' permission to live your life fully. Learn to let go and be willing to take what comes.

# *11* ~ JUSTICE

Justice represents our connection to the power of truth, balance, fairness, and harmony. The sword of truth stands in the middle to help discern positive from negative. Light, truth, clarity, lessons, and awareness of right action are revealed when Justice sifts through the details. Be clear about what you want to do, what you need to do, and what you can do. Use the higher function of wisdom to make decisions and be a force for good in your actions and choices. Remember that life is fluid and don't become too judgmental or closed off; then you will lead by example.

# *12* ~ HANGED MAN

The Hanged Man knows that life is full and often requires sacrifice and surrender to Spirit. *Sacrifice* means "to make sacred." Once you sacrifice or let go of your baggage, you will be lighter, more free. The Hanged Man helps you simplify, prioritize, relax, and let go of attachments to outcomes, the body, and selfishness. He holds the space for you to walk unknown paths, heal through crisis, and be an example to others through your humility. He is cheerful and not terribly concerned with mundane details. He depends upon his spirit for guidance, fully aware that life is one big cosmic play. He is also compassionate about the suffering of others. Be aware of your talent for procrastination. You can teach others by your ability to see that enlightenment comes in all forms and from every experience.

# *13* ~ DEATH

Death is the reaper, universally needed so that growth can occur. This archetype requires you to release old ways of being or thinking that no longer serve the higher good, allowing for the alchemy of your life—turning base metal into gold. Death often wears a crown representing higher consciousness. Death will guide you to become more compassionate and empathetic, and to develop a healthy appetite for appreciating life. Develop a trust that Spirit always renews, always restores. You are a catalyst for change and hold secrets of the Underworld. Be careful to not become too didactic, single-minded, or rigid, believing there is only one way.

## 14 ~ TEMPERANCE / ART / SOVEREIGNTY

Temperance holds the power of balance through the higher self integrating into our human self. This archetype helps others see the beauty and light within and grants the strength and confidence to be that beauty and light. It is the rainbow and promise of hope. Release others from expectations through a strong centeredness and sense of self and you will be an amazing and healed healer. Your ability to understand the value of the middle path helps you bring peace to situations where others are being extreme. Be careful not to tip the balance and become all work and no play. You have the ability to maintain angel awareness—the clarity of an uncluttered mind.

## 15 ~ DEVIL

The Devil is the spirit of positive rebellion and can represent ego. Often chains are shown in this card, holding us back. We need to listen to our heart to be free. The Devil shows us how to use external signs as messages that reveal our internal reality. The Devil helps you be creative and sensual, overturn negative influences through trickster energy, and see the pitfalls of relationships based on bondage and selfishness. The personality or ego helps you stand your ground and defend your beliefs, decisions, loves, and dislikes. Unguarded, the Devil represents the pride that will get in your way, the ignorance that will cloud your vision. Stay open to the freedom and ability to explore all possibilities; don't create imaginary limitations.

## *16* ~ TOWER

The Tower helps you give up what you thought was your identity, what you were supposed to be, so you can be what you truly are. Under the guidance of the Tower, the things you cling to most desperately, all the things you take for granted and believe you must remain attached to, fall away. You are forced to find an inner strength. Your defenses crumble so that the light of truth can strengthen you. The Tower symbolizes the possibility of rebuilding from a sense of your own beliefs and continually finding fresh and new ideas—a gypsy life of constant growth. Amazing awareness can come through lightning-flash insights. Remember that in the power of the moment, and you can get through any crisis with your natural courage.

## *17* ~ STAR

The Star represents a time to let your light shine. Live to your full potential. Relinquish any shame or fear—just be bright. Look inward to find your gifts and bring them forth. Here is the window of opportunity for the sweetness of life. Dream big! Believe you can attain the things you want—all is possible. The Star points to a time for meditation and inner reflection and symbolizes vulnerability and being willing to look deep within.

Be grateful for the gifts you will receive, for they will be many—both big and small. You've played out much karma and deserve the rewards. Practice mind over matter and tune into the stars and planetary movements. Be careful not to be impatient.

## 18 ~ MOON

The Moon represents unconscious behavior of the dreamworld rising to the surface. This archetype gives you the ability to watch emotions move and change and grants you the strength to walk through darkness without fear. This card speaks to the peace and compassion that come when the feral and tamed aspects within learn to work together in harmony. The Moon represents the emotions, illusions, or undercurrents that affect your daily life. A struggle and sometimes a little pain arises from evolving and shedding of old ways. Now is the time to deal with your karma and become aware of who you are. Be careful not to get stuck in your past. Separate fact from fiction so you will know when fears and doubts are clouding your vision.

## 19 ~ SUN

The Sun represents the glory of warmth and growth. It is the creative force at its finest. It is the harmony and ecstatic joy of dancing amidst treasures, the belief and experience of success and prosperity. What a time of bounty! The abundance of heaven has come to earth for you. Know that you are the Source and connect to the healing power of the Universe. Spread your joy and your sunny disposition, and teach happiness. Allow your openness to abundance to benefit all who come in contact with you. Be careful of apathy and becoming "sun-blocked" or bored; with an attitude of "everything is so good, so who cares," you can lose your ability to connect with life and people. Plus, you'll get burned if you don't appreciate what you have.

## 20 ~ JUDGMENT / AEON

Judgment represents the observer, one who can watch without becoming emotionally involved or lost. With the power of awareness comes the freedom and clarity to experience life without limits. Discernment (ability to make good decisions) and wisdom are gifts of this symbol. Turn your thoughtful perception inward and form a kind relationship with yourself. A more centered, more balanced you will emerge. With your courage to see things as they are, you have the ability to learn from experiences and liberate yourself from the pain of ignorance. Listen often to your own counsel; it will usually be very helpful and accurate for your own situation. Don't become overly judgmental or jaded.

## 21 ~ WORLD / UNIVERSE

The World represents a relaxing and rewarding life. It is the symbol of the victor bounding into the Spirit world. You have arrived and paid your karmic debts. Now it's time to appreciate life. Dance. Enjoy yourself. There is no separation between your higher self and your worldly self. You are in touch with all that is and see Spirit in all that you create. You can see the Divine in every day. But don't languish forever; there is always more to learn.

## 22 ~ FOOL

The Fool has absolute faith and trust, almost without fear of consequence, because eventually all *will* work out. The Fool is willing to embrace all experience and so holds the elements as playthings. The world is her playground. The Fool always lands on her feet, or at least views it that way. At the Fool's heart is innocence, openness, and adventure. This archetype is in balance with the earth and sky and holds an immense, trusting connection to all that is and limitless possibilities, with a strong belief in the future. Work on completing tasks and let go of the past.

Looking at how your year card works with your soul card is an interesting game to play. Two apparently opposite energies can and will coexist and affect each other. For example, the vanity of the Devil and the openness of the Lovers create complexity and conflict, but also an opportunity to find where the lines can be smoothed and harmony can reign.

The cards and archetypes represent the many facets of your inner self. You can call upon an archetype by placing the card on the refrigerator or on your makeup mirror. For example, if you need to break up with someone, you could call upon the powers of the Strength card. Keep in mind that the symbols on tarot cards represent only a skeleton or framework. You flesh it out by using what the symbols mean to you to see how it works and makes sense within the fabric of your life. Take some time to reflect on and write about what you learned about your soul and personality cards and the archetypes in the Major Arcana.

# Palmistry

Palmistry is a dynamic, ever-evolving art of divination. Did you know that the lines of the hand are not fixed and unchanging? The lines on your hand reflect your thinking, and as your attitudes, behavior, and thinking change, the lines physically change to reflect these changes. Amazing!

Trace your hand on the opposite page. Fill in the outline with symbols, words, colors, animals, or whatever you are drawn to write or draw. For symbol ideas, look on pages 18 to 24. For animal messages look on pages 15 to 63. Color associations are found on page 27.

## JUPITER FINGER

Also known as the pointer finger, Jupiter's finger rules over self-awareness, self-appreciation, power, and ego. Here you find traces of leadership and learn how you guide yourself and others. This finger is in charge of ambition, direction, and growth. The energy related to this finger corresponds to the general qualities of the god Jupiter, such as generosity and expansion.

## SATURN FINGER

Also known as the middle finger, Saturn's finger guards the space that lies between the conscious and the unconscious, the public and the private, and the outer and the inner. It creates the bridge between opposing sides of your nature. It rules over self-discipline, how you determine your worth and blessings, and how you see your position in life. This finger's energy also relates to the general attributes of the god Saturn, such as order and self-knowledge.

## APOLLO FINGER

Also known as the ring finer, Apollo's finger inspires your creativity. From this finger, a vein leads directly to your heart, so it is no wonder this finger reigns over love, romance, emotions, and your soul. It helps you identify your power, self-expression, talents, and gifts. It's related to the god Apollo and his reign over truth, medicine, music, poetry, and art.

## MERCURY FINGER

Also known as the pinky or little finger, Mercury's finger rules communication, intimacy, and relationships. It's interesting that the little one, symbolic of the details of your life, can have power over how you relate to others. This finger also directs travel and general motion, as does the god Mercury, who also rules over communication and is the patron of merchants.

## THUMB

Your will and force are centralized in the region from the tip of your thumb to the first knuckle. Here you find the determination to bring your desires to manifestation. The portion from the knuckle to your palm carries the energy of logic and reason and gives you the solutions you need to make your dreams come true. It's kind of like a tree trunk that provides the stability and foundation for the branches to do their thing.

## MOUNT OF VENUS

This region of the palm, located just under the thumb, rules love and desire. Here you find the ability to create beauty, joy, and laughter in your life. The energy of this section gets its power from the goddess Venus.

## LUNA OR MOON MOUNT

Ruled by the Moon, this is the meaty part of the palm under the Mercury finger, or the pinky. It is the center of your unconscious workings. Here you find your intuition, imagination, desire for personal freedom, and ability to change. It is ruled by the element water and carries all its graceful, mysterious nature.

## THE PLANE OF MARS

Found under the heart line and extending to the middle of your palm, the plane of Mars is divided into upper and lower sections.

The upper section, closer to the heart line, rules over your ability to objectively look at each situation in its own unique light. The lower section rules over aggression, assertiveness, and action. The basic energy of the plane of Mars is associated with the god Mars and his focus on drive, action, and courage.

Now take a look at the drawing of your hand you made a few pages ago. Think about how the meanings of the symbols, colors, animals, or words you wrote or drew connect to the meanings of the areas in which you drew them. For example, let's say you colored the Jupiter finger a sky blue color. And let's say that you view blue as a calming, centering color. One interpretation would be that you prefer to move ahead in a composed, confident, and peaceful way, or that you lead in a relaxed way.

This exercise lets you use symbols that are meaningful to you. It's up to you to discover the connections between the symbols and where you've placed them and to interpret what Spirit or your guides are saying to you. Write about whatever thoughts arise. You can do this exercise over and over again, but if you do, try not to think about what each area of the hand means so that you don't analyze during your creative process.

Palmistry often begins with testing of the texture of the hand. Is it supple? Rough? What does the feel of the hand tell you? There are several types of hand shapes. While these types offer a generalization, most people's hands combine several different types. The descriptions of hand types are sweeping, broad statements that should be measured against what you know to be true about yourself or the person whose hand you're reading.

Look at your hand shape and decide which of the various hand types you fit into. Take a look at the descriptions below and decide which elements or aspects of the hand shapes fit yours.

**The square hand** doesn't taper in the palm or fingers. The sides are parallel. This is often a practical, earthy, stable, hardworking person.

---

**The spatulate hand** is noted for wedge-shaped, flat fingertips and nails wider on top than at the cuticle. This person is often artistic, creative, considerate, generous, energetic, tenacious, and a humanitarian.

---

**The oval hand** is best known for its roughly egg-shaped palm, which ends at the wrist with a sweeping curve. This hand usually has slender fingers and oval nails. People with oval hands are sensuous, warm natured, a bit self-obsessed and self-indulgent, and in love with love and beauty.

---

**The oblique hand** has a rather long palm and fingers. Most of the fingers incline toward the Apollo or ring finger. People with oblique hands are often indecisive, quiet, methodical, and meticulous and move slowly to their own drummer.

---

**The knotty or philosophic hand** is best known for its pronounced joints or knuckles. Here are the great thinkers. These people know how to work and worry. They often possess a vivid imagination and are quite original in their ideas and philosophies.

Record any thoughts about your hand shape or what the characteristics of your hand, taken altogether, show about your nature.

# Athena's Animals

Many of the Goddesses have a consort, or familiar, an animal who guides, protects, and supports them. Athena, the Warrior Goddess, known for her protection, wisdom, and insight, has an owl. She's often seen wearing a helmet, holding a shield and sword, and with olive and oak trees. Diana, the Huntress, known for her strength and loyalty, has a dog. She's often seen with a bow and arrow, and since she is also a moon goddess, the moon casts its silvery light upon her. The Goddess of Spring Eostre, known for abundance, is always with a rabbit or hare. Eostre is usually surrounded by flowers, grass, and other signs of spring.

Look at the qualities and traits of the animals below. Choose an animal that you feel most like today, or one whose traits and powers you hope to have. If you can't decide on an animal, then write each animal name on a separate scrap of paper. Place the names in a bowl and draw out the name of an animal. Trust that whatever you pull out is no accident. Or set an intention to dream about an animal and see who comes to visit.

**BAT** represents rebirth, inner strength, fortune, and happiness. Bat will give you the power to overcome obstacles.

**BEAR** is a symbol of the need to rest, to hibernate. Through our quiet time we can heal, gain insight, increase intuition, and experience prophetic dreams.

**BEAVER** is a symbol of resourcefulness, security, achievement, and hard work.

**BUFFALO** represents the Great Spirit and is a symbol of abundance, prayer, alertness, and strength.

**BUTTERFLY** represents transformation, beauty, harmony, and the ability to accept change.

**CAT** represents cunning, independence, healing, love, enjoyment, and confidence.

**COUGAR** or mountain lion provides the power of leadership and encourages you to take responsibility for your life.

**COYOTE** is the trickster, who helps you recognize your own mistakes and learn to laugh at yourself. Coyote is the shape-shifter.

**COW** is a symbol of motherhood, fertility, and nourishment.

**CRANE** represents longevity and focus.

**CROCODILE** helps you with integrity, emotions, and discretion and empowers you to sift what's usable out of the heap.

**CROW** represents secrets, law, and intelligence and will bring you the ability to release past beliefs.

**DEER** represents gentleness, kindness, patience, and compassion. It's believed that the deer can carry you to Faeryland.

**DOG** represents loyalty, faith, devotion, and companionship. Dog will help you guard your territory.

**DOLPHIN** is all about play and laughter. Dolphin is also a symbol of life, breath, intelligence, and communication.

**DRAGON** represents prosperity, protection, magick, and intuition.

**EAGLE** is your connection with your soul and represents the ability to soar above and have a bird's-eye view. It helps you to see beyond the mundane to your higher purpose. The drawback is not touching down very often to connect with others.

**ELEPHANT** represents family and great affection and loyalty.

**ELK** or **STAG** represents endurance, patience, stamina, male essence, and passion as well as strength and courage.

**FOX** represents cleverness, patience, cunning, and the ability to wait for the right moment to act. Fox can teach you how to shapeshift or camouflage.

**FROG** represents fertility and cleansing tears and will help you make something wonderful out of a possible bad situation.

**HAWK** represents the messenger. Hawk's magick and strength will help you see meaning in mundane experiences.

**HORSE** represents freedom, power, and messages and brings friendship, journeys, and faithfulness.

**HUMMINGBIRD** is a symbol of pure joy. It will give you the ability to see beauty, love, and possibilities in everything.

**LION** represents wisdom and power and brings you skill in heart-centered leadership.

**LIZARD** represents the stillness of the dreamworld. Lizard is the guardian of the unconscious who brings into your awareness your subconscious hopes and fears so that they can be acknowledged.

**MOOSE** represents confidence, self-esteem, and wisdom. It will help you achieve through stamina.

**MOUSE** helps you notice the little things in life. Through scrutiny and attention to details you can be ever alert to the things going on around you.

**OTTER** is often seen as feminine energy and symbolizes creativity, magick, joy, friendship, playfulness, and curiosity.

**OWL** represents wisdom, clairvoyance, and magick and gives you the ability to see things that are normally hidden from view.

**PORCUPINE** represents humility, playfulness, trust, protection, faith, and innocence.

**RABBIT** symbolizes all our fears. Rabbit brings hidden teachings, quiet strength, quickness of thought and action, and comfort.

**RAVEN** is the messenger who helps you to see with keen eyes and clear perception. This bird represents prophecy and magick.

**ROOSTER** represents sexuality, watchfulness, and resurrection.

**SALMON** represents inner wisdom and knowledge. Salmon is a symbol of faith, fertility, journeys, and endurance.

**SNAKE** represents change, sensuality, and the ability to let go of things that are worn-out and no longer useful.

**SPIDER** represents Grandmother or Crone energy, harmony, infinite possibilities, creativity, trust, protection, and the weaving of fate.

**SQUIRREL** is a symbol of gathering and preparation. Squirrel encourages you to develop the ability to plan ahead and anticipate your future needs.

**SWAN** represents grace, dignity, and style and holds intuition and knowledge.

**TIGER** represents passion, sensuality, silence, solitude, and power.

**TURTLE** represents Mother Earth and gives you strength, patience, perseverance, stability, and the ability to center and pay attention to earthly things.

**UNICORN** represents possibilities, purity, magick, and truth. Unicorn gives you the ability to make your dreams come true.

**WEASEL** or ferret imparts stealth, foresight, and the ability to see beneath the surface of things to what the actual intent and meaning is.

**WHALE** symbolizes balance, music, family, and clairvoyance and is known as the keeper of the earth records (the history of Mother Earth).

**WOLF** represents your inner teacher and will help you to find your life path.

Now describe yourself as a goddess with her animal familiar. What symbols or images are you usually pictured with? Which animal is your consort and which of your familiar's qualities do you most represent? Add to the qualities of your animal guide. Tell the story of how you came to be and what you represent to the people who pray to you.

THE ENCHANTED DIARY

# Shape-Shifting

From time to time most of us create blocks to our success. One of the ways you can begin to defuse the energy of these blocks is to personify the energy that obstructs you and prevents you from living the life you choose. Name your fear and face it, and you can begin to transform the energy.

We always do what we really want to do. This is absolutely true. Our thoughts create everything we see and the way we see it. Even the obstacles that block you are really elements of your subconscious at work. What stands between you and the life you desire? You. That's all. So why aren't you living your dream life? There's a payoff to every situation we attract into our world. With creative shape-shifting, you can alter your fear or monster into something truly helpful. It's time to unravel those blocks and disengage their connections to your heart and mind.

Now light a black candle. You can unravel this mystery on either the full or dark moon. If the moon is waxing, or growing, focus on transforming the negative energy. If the moon is waning, or shrinking, focus on letting the negative energy go.

Imagine a girl your same age living in a small village where everyone has a talent, a place, a need they serve. The girl yearns to be great. She admires a strong woman who lived long ago. Her hero was a freedom fighter, a courageous woman who led armies to defend her people's land and their ways. Yet the girl lives in peaceful times, and there's no need for such a leader. She flops around in shoes too big for her feet and a desire too big for her heart to fill.

One day, the village elder had a vision of poisoned waters, concrete over meadows, and steel in the people's heart. The prophecy told of strangers crushing the beauty and peace of the land and her people. The strangers came, their lines stretching to the far reaches of the horizon.

The girl ran to a cave rumored to contain a special weapon. By the light of the full moon peeking through a hole in the cavern, she discovered a secret story written on the walls by the warrior princess of long ago. It foretold the coming of the war. Yet there would be hope in the form of a young girl with fire in her heart and courage in her soul. Her name would be. . . .

The girl stood incredulously staring at her own name. The writings described her perfectly. The warrior princess claimed she would be reborn as the next champion of the people. This time she would lead through her heart and prevail more fully than before. The girl and the women were one.

Most of us have some internal monologue that keeps us from standing tall in our light, something that prevents us from believing we can be our own hero. How would you feel if you discovered that a heroine you had worshipped was really you? How would it feel to suddenly know that you are already in possession of everything you value?

Breathe deeply three times. Close your eyes and hear the echoes of your own breathing and the water dripping from the cave's ceiling. Feel the cool, textured cave walls as you trace your name. In your mind's eye, imagine reading the description of your greatness, your courage, your kindness, and the great love the people hold for you. Suddenly your breath catches. Your toes turn cold and a little voice speaks of fear. Which of the following comments are most like your voice of fear?

**A** – Who the hell do you think *you* are?

**B** – It will never work, and it doesn't matter anyway.

**C** – What if you fall flat on your face?

**D** – I'm not strong, courageous, or good enough.

If you chose A, proceed to paragraph A. If you chose B, proceed to paragraph B. If you chose C, proceed to paragraph C. If you chose D, proceed to paragraph D. Look for a ringing, like an electrical current rushing through your body, trying to capture and extinguish your light. Eventually, read all of the paragraphs. Perhaps more than one monster speaks truth for you.

**A** – "Who the hell do you think *you* are?" demands the basilisk, a monstrous snakelike creature two stories tall. Cold, venomous green eyes stare at you with utter disgust. "What makes you think you can take all the glory? What a selfish beast you are. How dare you make the rest of us look bad while you strut around? You're not even that. . ." Write the rest of the basilisk's arguments in the space below.

_____

_____

_____

_____

_____

_____

**Inner Girl**　　　67

**B** – "It will never work," laments the sloth as he languishes, sprawling out his long arms. "No one will listen. Even if they did listen, the enemy is sure to crush you. It's Murphy's Law—something terrible always happens. More will be hurt. What if you never recover? Might as well keep the nasties in front of you where you can see them. Might as well stay safe and . . ." Write the rest of the sloth's arguments in the space below.

_____

_____

_____

_____

**C** – "What if you fall flat on your face?" crows the gargoyle as he preens his wings. "Ha! You'd look like a fool. You're half respectable now. But if you fail, you'll be a laughingstock. Even if you do succeed, everyone will expect you to be perfect all the time. Everyone will find out you can't cut it. Everyone will know you're weak. Everyone will know . . ." Write the rest of the gargoyle's arguments in the space below.

_____

_____

_____

_____

**D** – "You're not strong, courageous, or good enough," whimpers a microscopic infectious germ. "You don't know how to lead others. Let someone else do it. Look, you're shrinking right now. You don't deserve this. You've never succeeded before. Remember, the last time you tried this, it fell apart and you let everyone down. Remember when . . ." Write the rest of the germ's arguments in the space below.

_____

_____

_____

_____

Light dried, unbundled sage leaves and place them in a cauldron. Blow on the sage until the fire is extinguished and the sage smoke plumes into the air. As you blow, chant three times:

> I invoke thee, oh Cerridwen (Care-eh-dwin),
> Grandmother Crone, both wise and old.
> I invoke thee, oh Cerridwen,
> Transform base metal into gold.
> I invoke thee, oh Cerridwen,
> Show me my light, both bright and bold.

Get louder with each repetition. Either as you chant or in the silence that follows, imagine the monster that haunts you. See it rise from the ashes. With your mind's eye, watch Grandmother

Goddess Cerridwen reach out with her wand and tap the beast on the head. Watch the smoke envelop the monster.

If the monster was a basilisk, see it writhe and twist, hear it hiss angrily, and watch it transform into a great rainbow-colored lizard. Its eyes are now twin golden pools of unconditional support. The envy is totally gone. On the lizard's back is a huge heart.

He speaks to you: "My dear, I am so happy you have finally found the greatness within. Look at my rainbow. Can you see how each color shines? Each of these colorful expressions must first envision how it shines before it can do it. Dream. Imagine. Be as big as you can. I support your dreams, no matter how silly, small, or big they are. My support will never waver. When you see me lying out in the sun, know I stand guard in the dreamworld. I will help you and encourage you to dream. Your dreams are . . ." Write the rest of the lizard's wishes for you in the lines below.

_____

_____

_____

_____

_____

If the monster was a sloth, see it hold tight to the rock. Hear it groan contemptuously as it refuses to move. Watch waters rise to engulf it. Within the depths of the sea, the sloth grows from a skeptical, apathetic fiend to a strong, gentle blue whale. You sit on the rock and the whale rises to meet you.

"Failure is an illusion, my friend. I hold the records of all times. I have seen it time and again: there are no mistakes, only experience. You are magnificent, and yet even this grandeur is ordinary for you, as it is for everyone who expresses their true light. Believe. Be gentle with yourself and have faith in your convictions. You have a special gift to share. The world would be less bright without your light. Let me fill you up with the confidence, loyalty, and devotion I feel for you. Do not allow the illusions of negative possibilities be the only paints you use to color the canvas of your life. Like breath, you will always rise again. You can trust . . ." Write in the rest of the whale's wishes for you in the lines below.

_____

_____

_____

_____

_____

If the monster was a gargoyle, hear it squawk. Watch its hackles rise and see the gargoyle's worried look as it loses control over its form. The smoke blows through its feathers and lifts them into flight as the beast becomes a great eagle. With a proud, regal stare, the king of birds looks you dead in the eye.

"It is not your fate to be small. Nor do you serve or honor others by doing so. Honor your joys and desires, whatever they may be, because in exploring and feeling your bliss, you celebrate Spirit. And that is a celebration of life. You no longer have to be anything to prove yourself to me or anyone. Feel my power. Let me give you the grace and poise that have always been within you. Recognize yourself in the grand mirror I hold up. Let it feed your sense of self. Rise up and fly. It is safe to soar. Know that . . ." Write in the rest of the eagle's wishes for you in the lines below.

_____

_____

_____

_____

If the monster was a relentless, destructive germ, imagine the smoke encircling it. Watch the white smoke pump into the little bug, filling it with purified smoke. Hear the pop as the bug explodes. The smoke forms the shape of a great stag with an impressive rack of antlers. With gentle yet confident eyes, he speaks:

"Your gifts and talents are as numerous as the many prongs on my antlers. I have watched you since the day of your birth. You have accomplished more than you give yourself credit for. The fates have long ago envisioned your greatness. You met each challenge to the best of your abilities. You are quite capable. You are the seed of strength. I will support you as the earth supports the trees. Reach for the impossible, because for you, all is possible. You are worthy of great gifts, a life of ease, unconditional love. You will continue . . ." Write the rest of the stag's wishes for you on the lines below.

_____

_____

_____

_____

_____

Blow once more on the smoking sage. See your benevolent animal spirit merge with Cerridwen and change into a great big spider. With ancient eyes she looks at you, "Little one, I have lived many, many years. I have noticed how each strand affects my web. The same is true for everyone. We need everyone to be strong and true to their light for the web to be strong. Your fate is to be big and grand. You are beautiful. This is so."

Allow yourself permission to feel fully supported and capable. Believe in your strength and have faith in yourself. With this new mind-set you will dissolve the energy that blocks you. You will disconnect the web of energy that creates repeating patterns of sabotage, destruction, and dilution of your power. You will create a new attitude that supports you. You will no longer see accusations in the eyes of a stranger, friend, or family member, or even in your own reflection. You will see support for your dreams everywhere you look.

As with every magickal work, spell or otherwise, the effects take time to sink in and show themselves. You will need to do this visualization more than once for complete healing to take hold. Becoming whole is a process. How divided against yourself you are will determine how many times you need to repeat the visualization before it sinks in and you truly feel it's safe to rise to your potential. Try not to stay stuck regretting that you spent energy blocking your own success. That's a form of procrastination that will keep you from your greatness, too.

Eventually, you will bypass falling into the abyss of listening to the monstrous voices. Ultimately you will be able to hear the message of the benevolent animal spirit first and foremost. Everything that was once destructive can be transformed into a seed that creates something beautiful. That is the way of nature.

# UNIVERSAL INFLUENCES

While in our Enchantress years, ages thirteen to about thirty-three, we stand at a point of awakening to our immense power. Enchantresses hold a once in a lifetime belief in the vast possibilities of life. This concentration of unlimited energy attracts unexplainable moments from feelings of being hexed to sensing you've been touched by an angel. You are most likely to have mysterious moments during the Enchantress years because you are so open to the many options out there. You draw them like a magnet.

Have you ever walked down a street and felt strongly that you've been there before, even though you knew there was no possible way this could be true? Some people call that déjà vu. For some, the mystery is cool in of itself and there is no need to explore it further. Others want to dissect the mystery and find out why this new experience feels so familiar. As always, there are lots of possible reasons.

Many people believe reincarnation or past lives cause the mysterious familiarity for certain places or people. Earth is a school where we learn lessons (though you cannot pass or fail) and have the opportunity to experience situations from as many perspectives as possible. This allows us to feel the many expressions of the Divine. We often reincarnate with the same group of people, known as your soul family. So your mother could have been your sister or best friend in a past life. When you meet members of your soul family, you will feel totally connected without a logical reason. It's as if you've known them for lifetimes. You probably have.

Another possible reason for déjà vu relates to DNA memory. Our cells have intelligence. Let's say you were to fall out of a tree. As you fall, your whole body is on hyperalert. The cells located exactly where your body hits the ground will record the memory. Even after many years, you could press that spot just right and recall the smells and sounds just before impact. Since our cells are intelligent and we can pass on certain genes, say for blue eyes or curly hair, why can't we also pass on memories? The memories of our grandmothers may be passed along through our DNA.

Serendipitous moments may also be triggered by the collective consciousness, or the mind-set of humankind—the overall understanding of the people. For example, most people today believe the earth is round and revolves around the sun. It wasn't always that way. People used to believe that the sun revolved around the earth. Whether or not our planet is the center of the Universe affects how people view themselves.

Last, your dharma or karma could be what triggers uncanny coincidences. Dharma is living your life's purpose—that which will bring you peace of mind, inner strength, and true happiness. Karma is the law that for every action there is an equal reaction. Karma is the great balancer of energy in the Universe. If your life isn't in harmony with your dharma or if you're avoiding facing your karma, your spirit guides will push like a rogue wave to get you on the right track. This push begins gently, with chance meetings that could help you. If you don't see the signs, they will get increasingly obvious and eventually painful until you must change your ways to reflect the life you were meant to live.

For an example of dharma, let's say you go to nursing school because your father is a doctor and that's what he wants for you. However, at heart you're an artist, and the thought of a hospital makes you want to puke. Then, "coincidentally," some crazy lady shows up and offers you room and board if you'll be her artist apprentice. Follow the signs. Follow your bliss!

This chapter will help you figure out how to channel the power of the Universe to create a more powerful you. The information on the Indigo Children will give you an explanation for the intensity and feeling of needing a purpose that may course through you. The section on chakras and vortexes will help you to better tune into power centers within yourself and on earth. Ley lines and nadis will help you find a way to get into the groove and flow of life. Learning about the Aquarian Age will fuel your fire and give you the strength that comes from knowing you are fully supported to be yourself. Don't feel isolated by mystical events you may experience. Instead, use the information in this section to learn how influences ranging from concentrated earth energy to celestial movements to family history actually demonstrate the connectedness we share with everyone and everything.

# Indigo Children

Have you ever felt like you're on the wrong planet? The answer to why you feel this way may lie in the rainbow. Of the seven colors of the rainbow, only indigo can't be seen by the naked eye—indigo light travels so fast that we cannot see it. Indigo, which falls between blue and violet, is the color of the sixth chakra, and is located between your eyebrows. Also known as the third eye, this chakra rules over true sight and a centered inner vision that doesn't need to prove itself.

Indigo Children, spiritually advanced beings of light, see this kind of absolute truth. Your interest in magick and your willingness to claim your personal power tells me you are most likely an Indigo Child. Starting around 1980, a flood of people with high emotional or spiritual intelligence were born with the mission to help people create a safer and more loving life on earth. Indigo Children are known as spiritual warriors. They buck the system and demand explanations for things, ideas, or methods that most people take for granted as the "right" way. Indigo Children are system busters and will force change for the better.

Indigo Children, also called Star Children, speak about matters of Spirit and intuition with an otherworldly confidence that is often advanced beyond their years. They can often communicate telepathically. Earth's gravity may feel heavy and painful to an Indigo Child. They are so spiritually high that they sometimes forget the importance of grounding. If you feel this way, remember that you are not visiting earth as an etheric angel: you have been incarnated as a human being for a reason.

In about 1995, Crystal Children began coming to earth. These gentle souls are examples of a peaceful way of being. They are not easily ruffled, and they emanate pure, unconditional love. These children speak volumes with their eyes and often don't talk until after four or five years of age. Crystal Children and Indigo Children have a profound sense of purpose and feel a pressure to remember their earthly mission. Sometimes you may know very clearly why you came to earth and how you can help. Other times, the weightiness of this earth is literally painful and you wish desperately to just go home.

Let's create a mask. You can paint it to be an image of your inner self and empower it with the ability to know and accomplish your earthly mission. You can make it, put it on, and ask yourself what you are supposed to do here. You can draw or paint symbols of power on your mask (look on pages 18 to 24 for ideas) or design it to reflect the power of your element (try the elemental quiz on pages 5 and 6).

You will need a basic mask from a costume shop, liquid starch (available at craft stores and some grocery stores), newspapers, light cardboard, masking tape, a bowl, scissors, ear templates, and cardboard for ears. This is a messy technique. Remove rings, bracelets, and watches, protect the work area with newspaper, and wear clothes that are easily washed and that you don't care much about. Breathe deeply as you begin. Listen to your inner guidance for direction and inspiration. If you are drawn to work with the elementals, here are some suggestions: for air (sense of smell), make a prominent or unusual nose; for fire (sense of sight), make prominent or unusual eyelids; for water (sense of taste), make prominent or unusual lips; for earth (sense of touch), make prominent or unusual skin or hair; and, for all folk, Spirit (sense of hearing) can be represented by prominent or unusual ears. Traditional colors for the elements are bright yellow, bluish white, and pale colors for air; red, gold, crimson, and orange for Fire; blue, blue green, gray, and indigo for water; brown or green for earth; and clear, black, and white for spirit.

Tape the cardboard cutout of your chosen ears onto the back of the mask form, leaving the silhouette showing. Tear the newspaper into strips. Tearing creates an organic edge that blends into the whole better than a cut edge. The best length of strips for this project is about 3 to 4 inches. Dip one strip at a time into a bowl of diluted starch (1 cup starch to 2 tablespoons of water). Squeegee the strip between your fingers; the strip should be wet but not dripping. Lay it across your plastic mask either vertically or horizontally and smooth it down. Tear off any excess length and use it as a patch elsewhere. Dip another strip and put it on in the same direction, slightly overlapping.

For the ears, use small, short strips and wrap them completely around the cardboard both vertically and horizontally. After you've covered the entire mask, start the next layer in the opposite direction; so, if the first layer was vertical, or up and down, the next layer will be horizontal, or across. But be certain to add layers evenly to the entire mask. Six to eight layers make a strong mask.

Noses, eyebrows, lips, and hair can be added by soaking the strips of newspaper for a couple of minutes to make them extra soft. Then twist them up and place them on the mask. Eyelids and noses can be added with the light cardboard.

If you don't like to paint, you could collage your mask with colored tissue paper or light wrapping paper. The easiest technique is to rip the tissue or wrapping paper into pieces, then use a paintbrush to lightly cover the entire mask with thinned white glue and put the pieces on. Paint over the entire mask with the thinned glue to smooth the edges. Also consider using crayons, markers, glitter glue, fabric, feathers, buttons, or shells. Look around for odds and ends to add uniqueness to your mask. Add elastic to hold it on your face. You can paint the elastic to match either the mask or your hair.

Write about your thoughts while making the mask.

THE ENCHANTED DIARY

# Chakras and Vortexes

Spinning wheels of concentrated energy exist throughout all aspects of the Universe, from a spiraling galaxy or orbiting moon, to tree trunks and the patterns of a blossom unfolding, to vortexes on Mother Earth and chakras in the human body.

The chakras are often referred to as spiraling flowers or focal points of energy. They vibrate with specialized powers or energy at specific regions in the body. There are seven main chakras where we receive, understand, and send out energy. For example, through our heart center, the fourth chakra, we accept love, absorb love into our being, and then give love out to the world.

The first chakra located between your sitting bones is red and grounding. We experience it primarily during the childhood years as we begin the process of grounding our spirits into this earthly realm. Any of us could have chosen to visit earth as a benevolent spirit; however, we chose to incarnate into a human body for a human experience. During·the first seven years of life, the process of understanding survival and what it means to be flesh and bones begins.

The Enchantress gains much of her power from the second and third chakras. The second chakra is bright orange and is located at the lower belly at the genitals. The sacral chakra, as it is known, processes experiences that help us understand duality and deepen our unique identity, creativity, and sexuality. Within duality there is dark and light, death and life, yin and yang, female and male. We learn that every situation has two sides and figure out where we stand on a multitude of issues. We awaken to our sexuality and hopefully learn that it is sacred and pure when it is honored and used in healthy ways. The second chakra, fueled by our female energy, ignites our ability to create, inspire, and be inspiring.

The third chakra is yellow and is located just above the belly button. The solar plexus, as it is often called, concerns itself with will and power. Here we learn the extent of our will and discover ways to fine-tune our determination to get what we need and want. We learn how we act when we have power and how we act when we don't. This chakra uncovers our resolve to share our talents with the world. Here you find your gut intuition and the drive to follow it.

The fourth chakra, located at the heart, is green or sometimes pink and concentrates its energy on unconditional love. It is linked to Mother Energy. If your heart is blocked, you will not be able to receive love or truly assimilate kind words into your consciousness. You must make sure your heart center is always open, no matter how many times you get hurt.

The fifth chakra, located at the throat, is blue and focuses on your ability to speak and communicate. Learn to speak your truth in ways that honor your integrity but that can be heard by others. Your voice must rise up and come out. Keep your throat chakra open so you can speak your truth and share your gifts with the world.

The sixth chakra, found in your forehead just above your eyes, is indigo. This is your third eye, and it has the ability to see beyond time and space. With the Crone's wisdom, it allows you to see into the future or the past and perhaps even get images of things happening somewhere else. This third eye composes all the information it receives into a single laser beam of knowing.

The seventh chakra, or the crown chakra, is located at the crown of your head and glows bright white. This energy center serves as a doorway for you to receive Divine inspiration. It is through this energy center that we connect to all that is.

Close your eyes and take three deep breaths. Think about the seven chakras. Imagine each chakra in turn, visualizing its color. Become aware of the flexible range of expansion and constriction within each energy center. If a chakra feels tight, don't get caught up in analyzing why, just tell the muscles or the chakra to open up. Stay with each chakra until it feels strong before moving on to the next one. When you've worked your way up through the seventh chakra, take three deep breaths once again. Focus on your breath and clear your mind. Try not to imagine or see anything.

Once you're relaxed, ask yourself which chakra is your center of being. In other words, where is your core? Where do you feel safe? Go with the first thing that pops up. Record your experience in writing or with art. What does it mean to be centered at this chakra? How does it help you?

THE ENCHANTED DIARY

Now close your eyes and take three deep breaths once again. Ask yourself where your center of power is. Again, don't second-guess yourself. How do you use your center of power? What happens when it's blocked?

_____

_____

_____

_____

_____

_____

_____

_____

_____

_____

_____

_____

_____

_____

_____

_____

_____

_____

_____

_____

Chakras can amplify, mute, or distort incoming information based on whether they are open, closed, or engorged. An engorrged chakra means you've got too much focus here, and it needs to mellow out. Through awareness of your chakras, you will be able to fine-tune your ability to understand situations clearly using your innate intuitive abilities of clairvoyance (clear seeing), clairsentience (clear knowing), clairaudience (clear hearing), or clairessence (clear smelling). See pages 12 to 17 to discover where your intuitive talents lie.

Just as the human body has chakras, where energy is concentrated, Mother Earth has areas of intense energy known as vortexes. Vortexes are spinning wheels of energy that serve as portals. They exist in special locations such as the red rocks of Sedona, Arizona; Mayan ruins on the Yucatan Peninsula; and the sacred land of Jerusalem.

Often the energy at vortex sites is frenetic or chaotic. That's the spiral energy working to call up all the dark and unhealed places within you. Just being in a vortex area can drum up painful experiences and bring them to the light of love and healing. Alternatively, you may feel boundless joy. Some people see actual doorways at vortex sites; others see auras or glowing light just above the landscape.

Vortexes aren't confined to specified locations. There are portals or openings for healing everywhere, even in your hometown. When I was nineteen, I was seemingly on a mission to leave this planet. I got into four car accidents in just five months, each worse than the one before. In one of the accidents, it was just beginning to rain when I hit a groove in the road. I pulled the steering wheel to the right and found myself headed directly toward an on-ramp that rose sixty feet above the ground, so I swerved back to the left. I went into a tailspin, spinning across the freeway from the slow lane to the fast lane. Miraculously, no car hit me, which was odd since I had been surrounded by traffic just moments before.

I slumped against the steering wheel unhurt. Suddenly I felt as though someone was trying to get my attention. I looked up, and through the drizzling rain across the freeway, I saw a man jumping up and down and pointing. I looked behind me and saw my car was on fire. I looked back across the freeway, but the man and his car were gone. Where was he? Then another man drove up with a hose attached to his truck and doused the flames. He parked in the fast lane, but no one hit him. Then, just to solidify the experience, a policeman came by and gave me a ticket for going "too fast for the conditions of the road." An interesting line that served to make the situation helpful and real. I couldn't discount anything, and every detail stood out crystal-clear. The policeman left, and soon afterward a tow truck showed up and gave me a ride home. I was a bit dumbfounded.

Whenever I pass this section of the freeway, I'm drawn back into the experience. This place is a vortex for me, and through this opening, I see and feel complete confidence that even during my darkest times, a host of angels and guides is working overtime to protect me.

Sedona, Arizona is a place well known for its vortexes (the hotels sell maps to the different vortex sites). In Sedona the trees' trunks often twist in a spiral, guided by the swirling energy of a vortex. Cities or areas that are filled with vortexes will also draw many spiritual healers to live in their midst. The vortexes feed spiritualists and metaphysicians the energy they use to heal their clients. Through the doorway of a vortex we see our connection to Spirit and the light that heals all.

Take some time to reflect upon and write about doorways in your life where you have experienced a change of heart. You might discount your "woo woo" moments because they don't seem big enough: there was no music, no bright swirling lights; the world didn't seem to stop. Spiritual experiences often seem small and are ignored or disregarded as insignificant. And please don't feel bad if you think you haven't had any. You probably have, and with some attention you will recognize it the next time it happens.

# Nadis and Ley Lines

Invisible lines of focused energy exist within our bodies. They are known as nadis or meridians (*nadi* is a Sanskrit word meaning "river" or "stream"). Estimates of the number of nadis differ, but it's said there are anywhere from 72,000 to 300,000 lines of energy coursing through our bodies. In their grid of light, these rivers maintain our energy flow and are responsible for movement.

There are three particularly important nadis: the ida, pingala, and sushumna. The ida, on the left side of the body, is white and is generally associated with the moon, prana (rising vital breath), semen, and Shiva (male). The pingala, on the right side of the body, is red and is generally associated with the sun, apana (descending breath), blood or ovum, and Shakti (female). The sushumna is in the center of the body and is the highway for the chakras. Connection to the sushumna nadi brings supreme consciousness.

You can break through dams of pent-up energy in the nadis in several different ways. One way is through yoga. Through the stretching and deep breathing, your vital breath pushes through the blockage. This release of energy can make you feel light-headed, at one with all living beings, ecstatic, or all three. Often the release is accompanied by a flood of tears or a burst of laughter. Or even a fart. I swear.

As with chakras and vortexes, the nadis in the human body are paralleled by key lines in Mother Earth. Like a mysterious faery chain, ley lines are alignments that stretch across the landscape to connect ancient sites. Alfred Watkins first coined the term *ley lines* in 1924 to describe the powerful, invisible earth energies that connect various spiritual and magickal locations such as churches, temples, stone circles, vortexes, burial sites, holy wells, and sacred groves of trees. Trails of sacred pilgrimages or journeys often follow key lines. Scientific and metaphysical evidence proves energy grids and lines crisscross the globe. One ley line connects the standing stones in the United Kingdom, while another is an invisible path leading to Montserrat Monastery in Spain.

The way these energy lines work is similar to how sound or light waves carry information. For example, a certain place could carry the vibration of the sun because the site stands above a ley line connecting sacred sites where rituals celebrating the solstice have taken place for years, perhaps centuries. If you walk on that site or line, both you and a friend might immediately think of the sun, bright and glorious. Has something like that ever happened to you, where you just entered a room, meadow, mountaintop, wherever, and you and another person had the same thoughts? If you give power and value to these experiences, they'll increase with your awareness. Some people would dismiss this experience as mere coincidence. Coincidences are magick at work. Another way to think of coincidence is as coinciding incidences that happen at the same time, drawn together by the magnetic force of light for the purpose of healing.

Write about any experience where you came into a space that seemed to drip with coincidence.

# Aquarian Age

Back in the sixties, when the hippies stormed the street burning bras, calling for peace, and advocating free love, the general populace thought they were crazy. Visionaries are often thought of in that way, as lunatics. But since one definition of *lunatic* is "one who worships *la luna*" (the moon), that's not a bad rap, actually. The hippies merely responded to a call. The Age of Aquarius had dawned and they celebrated it.

An age or era lasts approximately 2,500 years. During an age there is a particular kind of energy or influence that gathers its qualities and unique makeup from an astrological sign. The Piscean Age, which began approximately before Jesus was born, was a time when the major influence encouraged people to transcend the self, to find meaning in life. In the zodiac, Pisces is the sign of the mystic, and the Piscean age is characterized by dreaminess, symbolism, sensitivity, and intuition. It's represented by a fish (think of the Christian fish), but the Pisces symbol is of two fish, connected yet swimming in opposite directions. The Age of Pisces was ruled by duality. We sought spirituality by looking outside ourselves. We became separate from God, even though Jesus, Buddha, and other great teachers taught that God lived within us. It was a time to explore consciousness and the unknown. We learned to be chameleons, to be sympathetic, and to develop our emotional intelligence—our psychic abilities.

Then came the radical, revolutionary Age of Aquarius. This is a time for rebellion, assertion, and awakening to the power within, a time to defend individuality, freedom, and personal space. It is about knowledge, intelligence, equality, and pure, uncompromising truth. The Aquarian influence causes people to explore, experience, question authority, scrutinize and evaluate the effectiveness of the current system, and seek a system that supports self-governing and personal responsibility. It encourages a more holistic approach to life. The Aquarian energy inspires original thought, optimism, creativity, and curiosity. The Aquarian Age began to subtly affect the collective consciousness, or the mind-set of the world as we entered the Age of Industry. The booming of the technology industry was just the slightest hint of the Aquarian Age that would grow to shake the foundation of society and world consciousness in the sixties.

The task of those alive today is to seek out the gems of the Piscean Age and find a way to blend them into the Aquarian Age. When you take seemingly opposing energies and bring them close together, the space between them comes alive with thousands of possibilities. It's like dumping blue paint into a bucket of yellow paint and watching in fascination as a unique shade of green emerges.

Use the space on pages 96 and 97 to create a bridge in your own life that connects the dreamy, emotional Piscean state with Aquarian idealistic independence. Show the evolution from Piscean to Aquarian with colors, words, or animals, or write a story or poem of a utopian community that has the best of both worlds. Or, take one aspect of yourself and show how you've taken the best of past behaviors and carried them into your future.

THE ENCHANTED DIARY

# GODDESS HERSTORY

Istory is "his story." *Herstory* is our story, the tale of evolution of the Goddess. Our story is one of support, love, struggle, survival, and celebration. Many people would say that we've had war since humankind's beginnings. However, if you were to ask a woman, she might answer differently. After all, women have been tending relationships, feeding, loving, nurturing others, and developing themselves for thousands of years. "War? I suppose," she might say, "but did you see the beauty of the rainbow this afternoon or hear this great joke?" Herstory is ripe with hope, love, and laughter.

In modern society, we rarely celebrate entering each phase of womanhood, nor is there a distinct support system where one face of the Goddess champions the other. Instead, we see competition and morphing of one archetype into another, rather than celebrating the gifts of each phase of the Goddess in turn. For the Divine Feminine to rise to her full power, as she must, we must harken back to the times and ages when women supported one another. It is time to break the patriarchal belief system that women are out to hurt each other and to remember our innate nature of support and unconditional love.

As a young woman, it is so important that you understand there is a long line of powerful women supporting you. Undo the damage done by history and the labels of shame. Regardless of what rules or boxes society would put you in, remember that you are innately blessed and strong. Have you ever looked into two mirrors reflecting one another to see a seemingly endless line of images of yourself? Try it. Imagine those images to be a lineage of strong and able women who constantly support and pray for you to be the strongest, brightest light you can be. The ones who gaze back at you are midwives who fought to maintain dignity during birth, suffragists who fought for our right to vote, and women's libbers who fought for our right to work. In those women you will see blue eyes just like yours or the brown skin of your ancestors. However, if the mirror could go back to the beginning of time, that first face would be dark brown for everyone. Human migratory patterns and archaeologists have proven it. We are all descendants of the motherland, Africa. We are all related. So let go of your prejudices and feelings of envy or sabotage. We are all one.

You are woman—what does your roar sound like? What do you look like when you express your bold and beautiful self? Use this section, our Goddess herstory, to remember and honor your place within the Divine. This recognition alone will help bring the world back into harmony.

The section on moon lodges and red tents will help you restore your sacredness. Once you learn how Eve was framed, you can set her and yourself free of shame and guilt. Understanding Demeter and Persephone will give you a guideline for how to accept, seek out, or appreciate women who support you. Belly dancing puts the fun, personal strength, and majesty back into being sacred and sexy. The section on magickal mentors helps you discern who would be a good teacher. If we can remember our strength and birthright as powerful women—emotional and intuitive, not just logical—we will restore peace in the hearts of all and change the world.

# Moon Lodges and Red Tents

When I first started my period I was mortified. It was already insulting enough that I got boobs years before my friends, now this! Ugh. I spotted on white pants (who knew you couldn't wear white pants on those days?). I tried to explain it was the pizza from the cafeteria. Problem was, pizza wasn't served that day. I had the curse, as it used to be called. Whether the curse was to be a woman or to get your period, I wasn't sure. From then on, any time I was in a bad mood, I heard "Are you on the rag?" If this is the beginning of all life, why is it so embarrassing? There had to be another way.

It actually wasn't until a few years ago that the gift of a woman's menses sank in. I began my period on the day I was to receive my Native American name in a very special, ancient ceremony. I had fasted all day and meditated on my friend's name, and she had done the same for me. I knew I would have to tell the group I was on my period because...well, I just knew. Once I told them, I was forbidden to create the medicine wheels, gather herbs, or even be in the circle for the tobacco blessing. It still felt like the curse, and that hurt. A Native elder pulled me aside to explain.

"Women are the givers of life," he said. "It is because of the ceremony you go through every month that life exists for any of us. Your ceremony is so sacred, so blessed, that we will not diminish its importance by having you do two ceremonies at once. You are not being punished, but honored." Now there's a different take. "Women are so powerful," he continued. "During their moon time, they could affect the entire ceremony to meet their personal needs, which doesn't serve the community."

I have since discovered the book *The Red Tent*, which describes women's life during the Old Testament times and how they honored their female cycles. All the women bled at the same time, which tends to happen when women are close. These women secluded themselves in a tent, away from the menfolk and children. The elder women or young girls prepared the meals and took care of the chores. The women of the red tent hung out together and honored their ceremony as sacred. In North America, women of native cultures gathered in the moon lodge so that they could rest and recycle what no longer served them. They, too, had their needs taken care of by the others so that they could be present to their monthly ritual.

What would it be like if when you were buying tampons or pads at the store and the clerk called over the loudspeaker that he needed a price check for the scented pads with wings, you didn't cringe or wish the ground would swallow you up, but could stand there tall and proud? "Yep, I'm on my moon. Pretty cool, eh?"

I have participated in many rituals for young women to honor the beginning of their moon cycle. The ceremonies are simple. You could easily create your own by making red beaded jewelry or wearing red clothes to making magickal tools and musical instruments from items found in nature. Whenever I'm on my moon, I pamper myself—I don't cook or exercise. Cramping is far less, and for me the actual bleeding is about half of what it used to be.

Our sacred blood not only represents life, it represents courage, passion, sexuality, and strength. Consider what you can do for yourself to honor and celebrate your moon cycle. If you or a friend has not yet entered the world of womanhood, plan a ceremony to honor this when it happens. Write about how you can take time out for yourself to make this monthly ritual more pleasant and rewarding. What can you do to honor the fact that you are a woman?

THE ENCHANTED DIARY

# Eve Was Framed

The story of Eve and Adam as it is known today devalues women. I was ten when I first heard it told. I was sitting on the couch during a Christian Bible study class that latchkey kids went to instead of going home. When the woman said men rose from the dust of the earth, I giggled quietly. What was she trying to pull, I wondered? I was raised to believe that Father/Mother God created humans directly from thought. Then she said woman came from the rib of man, and I lost it. I fell off the couch laughing hysterically. I thought she was telling some wicked joke. This was during the height of the women's movement, and there was no way I could believe that from the very start woman was subordinate to man.

I was asked to leave, which I did gladly. I didn't even hear the whole snake and temptation bit, which probably would have incited me beyond reason, my little Chicana head wagging back and forth with a slew of rebellious insults. I know now that the tree from the Garden of Eden represents the World Tree, Ygydrasil, the Tree of Knowledge. I wonder, how can it be considered evil that we ask each other to look at knowledge, to consider all things? The snake represents transformation, death, and rebirth. Is it possible that woman asked man to look beyond what he could see, to look for what he could understand and feel rather than prove by his five senses? That is not a sin, but the gift of the Divine Female!

The legacy of Eve is not for women to take on the blame for all eternity, to see Eve as responsible for all the sins of womankind and believe that we ourselves are shamed, or to bear the weight of oppression. Eve asks only that we take from life the richness, the juicy apple. She has waited patiently in the dark and through the ignorance for women to realize their worth. The time has come to cast off the shackles of our self-imposed prison. Eve was a temptress, true. But the Temptress is a facet of the Goddess. In fact, you represent that very aspect of the Goddess during this period of your life. The Temptress is responsible for the holy, blissful feeling of riding a roller coaster during that first kiss. Don't punish or exploit the Temptress within you. Don't make her shamed because society is afraid of being too free.

The Temptress loves her friends, so allow a goddess sister to help free Eve from her entanglements. Freya, the Nordic Goddess of Lust, is just the right goddess. Wearing a falcon cloak and an amber necklace, Freya rides a chariot led by a leopard through the Milky Way. She is in charge of keeping sensuality alive and collecting fallen Vikings and carrying them to a special place in heaven.

During the evening on a Friday (named after Freya), place red stones around a red candle for Eve. Add a bright red apple to the altar. Add anything that reminds you of Eve, such as a fig leaf or a picture of a snake. Also place orange stones or crystals (amber or even tree sap if possible) around an orange candle. Add anything that reminds you of Freya, such as a feather or a picture of a leopard or falcon.

Women need to be free to be women—powerful, strong, and beautiful. The Temptress, also known as the Enchantress, is as sacred as any face of the Goddess. She's the force that pushes us to try new things. She gives us fire and courage when we need them. Light your red and orange candles. Allow a low hum to begin in your throat. Focus on the "m" part. Then release an "ah" sound. "Mah" is a primordial sound used in virtually every culture since the beginning of time to represent the Mother, the Goddess, and the Divine Feminine. Chant slowly, gathering power in the "mah" sound. Visualize Eve bound in chains. With your mind's eye, watch as Freya unloosens one chain and then watch Eve find the power within to release herself from the rest of her bonds. Say

*Eve is powerful; Eve is free.*
*This I make true three times three times three.*
*I am powerful; I am free.*
*This I make true three times three times three.*
*Freya is sacred, sexy, and free.*
*This I make true three times three times three.*
*I am sacred, sexy, and free.*
*This I make true three times three times three.*
*By My Will so Mote It Be!*

Record your thoughts about this ritual and getting to know Eve in a new way.

# Demeter
# and Persephone

Once upon a time, there was a beautiful young Goddess named Kore—the Spring Goddess. Fair and bright was she, with long golden hair and a ready smile. She enchanted the bees to buzzing and the flowers to growing with her grace and kindness.

One day Kore's mother, Demeter, the Grain Goddess, lovingly watched her daughter walk through the tall grass and knee-high wildflowers. The sun shot his warm golden rays to the earth, illuminating cobwebs and faeries' dances. Kore spotted a beautiful white flower she had never seen before. When she plucked the flower, the ground opened up, revealing a spiral staircase.

Kore gathered her skirts and descended down the spiraling stairs. The dank smell of earth wrapped itself around her, and gems of every color of the rainbow lit her way. At the bottom of the stairs, an underground lake lapped gently. A handsome, dark man sat upon a throne on the opposite shore, flanked by gnomes, centaurs, and creatures Kore had never seen before. "Welcome to the Underworld. I am Hades. Come."

Kore bravely approached the King of the Underworld, walking on stones that magickally appeared on the lake with each step she took. Ghosts of the dead whispered in her ear as she passed. The gray coldness of the place cloaked Kore like a wet blanket. By the time Kore reached Hades, a full banquet of the most delicious dishes sat before him.

"Please eat with me," Hades begged.

Kore faltered, unsure if this was wise.

Hades held up a turquoise bowl. "Perhaps some pomegranate seeds?"

Meanwhile, the sun rose many times while Demeter awaited her daughter's return. Demeter abandoned the field she had tended so carefully to search for Kore. The harvest failed, grapes shriveled on the vines, and the earth became barren and cracked. Demeter became as tattered looking as a beggar woman—not at all like a goddess.

"Something must be done to aid Demeter. Has no one seen Kore?" asked Zeus, Father of the Gods.

"I saw her descend into the depths of the Underworld," replied Helios, the Sun God.

Zeus looked worried. Anyone who drank or ate in the Underworld would be bound to live there always.

Kore reached out for the turquoise bowl. She popped six seeds into her mouth. The seeds exploded with tangy flavor. The crimson color reminded Kore of the blood that sustains all human life, and the drabness of the Underworld faded from her sight. Instead, she came to recognize Hades' kingdom as the source for the seeds' birth. "I am no longer Kore, the little daughter, but Persephone, Queen of the Unborn," she proclaimed.

Hecate, the wise Crone Goddess, decided that Persephone, as she was now known, belonged in both worlds and that Persephone's power was to bridge the worlds of the living and the dead. She would remind the living to be joyous and show the dead the way to rebirth. For each of the six seeds she had eaten, Persephone lives a month in the Underworld with Hades. During that time her mother, the Grain Goddess, cries, bringing cold rains, and retreats, and in her mourning nothing grows. We call these seasons autumn and winter. But when Persephone returns to earth, Demeter is overjoyed. Together, the two Goddesses coax flower faeries, vegetables, fruits, and trees into growing and blooming profusely. These are the seasons we know as spring and summer.

Like Persephone, each of us encounters tests along the way. Even if it's not a formal engagement or ceremony, we constantly undertake rites of passage to claim our identity. Perhaps none is as great as the coming of age during our teen years. Consider when you have been challenged and how you rose to the occasion to claim your unique path as right and perfect for you. Where did you walk through the valley of the shadow of death? Write about your heroic journey to the light.

Some of us are supported by women of older generations; others are not so lucky. Try to imagine that your mother is akin to Demeter, truly lost without your beauty, joy, and love reminding her how to live freely. Know you are loved beyond measure.

If this is too difficult for you, then visualize the archetype of Mother and Crone loving and supporting you. You may see her as Demeter, Gaia, Isis, Mother Mary, Hecate, Kali, or another. Use whatever creativity calls to you in this visualization. For example, you might make a piece of jewelry to place on an altar as a gift for your supporting guide and make a matching piece for yourself. Or try writing or creating a collage about the connection you share. Use the next page to express your feelings about your support system. There is no need to feel alone when love surrounds you like the air you breathe.

# Belly Dancing

Some people and cultures include the Enchantress in the Maiden face of the Goddess. I choose to call out the Enchantress as her own face of the Goddess because her challenges are unique and separate from those of the child. With the start of her menses, she takes on greater responsibility than the lighthearted Maiden. Her sexuality is born and she must learn how to channel it. The Enchantress is the fourth face of the Goddess. While three is a magickal number of manifestation, four represents equality and balance—qualities needed to empower the women of today.

Magick begins with the understanding that you are the Divine. You are the mystery of the night, the beauty of a rose and its sharp thorns, lilting dolphin's laughter, the eternity of a mountain, the curve of a pear, silver moonbeams, and the womb of all creation. You are woman and you are beautiful. You are a goddess.

Women need to recognize the power of our beauty, the grace of our movement, and how that can feed our energy, not deplete it. In Western cultures, the perception of belly dancing has morphed, becoming less a celebratory dance among women and more of a spectator sport. Truly, it was born out of the home, a social dance where grandmothers and mothers taught daughters. Cousins, aunts, and all the women joined in the celebration. The dance has evolved so much that its origins are highly debated. It has been reported to originate from Turkey, Morocco, Algeria, Iraq, Iran, Greece, Syria, Jordan, Lebanon, and Egypt, also known as the mecca of belly dance today.

In its pure form, belly dancing is an expression of the joy of living, being playful and focused with body movement, and sharing Spirit. Some movements awaken the spiritual connection between the physical and spiritual bodies. The pure joy and pleasure that arises from dancing for yourself creates what is known amongst belly dancers as "the feeling." When a dancer who is performing for others is able to convey that inner bliss and connection with her dance and body, she is said to have the feeling. The most wonderful aspect of the feeling is that it emanates from women of all shapes, sizes, and ages. Beauty as we usually think of it is not a prerequisite to the feeling, but beauty is born of that joy bubbling over. In the Middle East, the oldest belly dance stars are often the most revered and are loved and honored well beyond their retirement from the stage.

Belly dancing is not as easy as it looks. It takes practice and concentration. It asks you to draw on your feminine energy to move in mastery of your body and your power. With belly dancing, you discover your power is a self-fulfilling act and not something you must rely upon another to give you. Belly dancing is regal, sensual, joyful, and unapologetic. As intended, it is a reminder that you are capable of anything you set your mind to.

If you were standing in your true power, strong and capable, what would your life look like? Power develops with integrity, and a true honoring of yourself and others is beautiful. You can be beautiful, sexy, and sacred just for the feeling it gives you, not for anyone else. Record your dreams of standing in your full power as a beautiful, masterful woman. What are you doing? What do you look like? Who is there? You can write or paint or make a collage to express your experience.

In belly dancing, a relationship between the dancer and the audience is created. The more receptive the audience, the more energy is fed to the dancer. The more the dancer feels joy, the more she feeds the audience with her delight and pleasure. At a Hafla, or party of belly dancers, women gather and dance for one another, sharing the joy of the dance.

Practice with the experience of giving energy by sitting with a friend. Face each other with your eyes closed. Place your palms face down on your friend's hands, held face up. Ask your friend to clear away any thoughts and remain as open as possible. Think of a wonderful experience or idea that brings you joy and pleasure. Visualize that energy leaving your heart or wherever it shines from and streaming toward your friend. Continue to practice sending energy for a while. Switch when you're ready.

Sending energy, whether through spells, visualizations, or prayers, is the first step in establishing the life you want to live. The Universe will comply when you send direct and clear energy. Record your thoughts on sharing energy with another.

_____

_____

_____

_____

_____

_____

_____

_____

_____

# Magical Mentors

Mentors are an important aspect of growing wise and magickal. Mentors may not be presented as we think they should appear. Their religion or spiritual beliefs may differ from yours. They may do things differently and dress differently. In fact, you may have more to learn from them precisely because they are different. And if your mentors are truly wise, they will learn from you too.

A mentor essentially brings out the best in you and assists you in achieving your potential. Mentors help you develop confidence and grow stronger. You don't have to love or even like them. But you will learn to respect them. Mentors will assist you on your path and also give you the space you need to deepen your experience of yourself. If someone you think of as your mentor asks you to do something outside of your ethical stance, it's important to speak from your heart and hold your truth. You must be able to live with yourself and the consequences.

Mentors are not necessarily old people, they're just people with something to share, or who can hold a space for you to grow and give you unconditional love and support. They make sure you are grounded so you can reach for the heavens. Mentors will be patient, loving, kind, understanding, intelligent, vulnerable, down-to-earth, brutally honest, safe, supportive, and able to hold appropriate boundaries.

If you already have a mentor, write about how she or he has influenced your life. If you don't have a mentor, light a white candle and call in all the attributes you would like your mentor to have. Create a ritual using the elements corresponding to the type of mentor you want to manifest. You may want a motherly mentor, in which case use symbols corresponding to water. You may want a crone, or grandmother, in which case use symbols corresponding to earth. Elemental correspondence are found on pages 18 to 24.

# RITUALS AND SPELLS

Rituals, visualizations, spells, meditations, affirmations, and prayers are all essentially the same thing. They all consist of setting aside time and energy to focus on creating your desires and needs or releasing those things, people, and ideas that no longer serve your highest good.

What does the phrase "no longer serves your highest good" mean? It means that a method of behavior that used to help you now harms you. For example, if you grew up with a critical mother, you may have learned to keep a fair distance between you and loved ones or authority figures. That served your highest good at one point. It may have been exactly what you needed to preserve your sanity or independence. But as you grow older and encounter trustworthy, gentle people, the distance only serves to keep you isolated and blocked from developing bonded, caring relationships.

You can use rituals, spells, and visualizations to make dreams come true or deal with life's tough issues. Magick is play. It's a physical representation of an emotional need. We light candles, play with crystals, and chant to show Spirit what we desire. Rituals, prayers, and visualizations set your intent for your journey. They create dreams, abolish nightmares and empower you and place you at the steering wheel of your life.

It may seem overwhelming that every time you concentrate on a need, it begins to find a path toward manifestation and appearing in your life. But that's how the whole phrase "be careful what you wish for . . ." came into being—it's true. Luckily for us, the elementals and Goddess/God are here to help. Your world is unfolding as it should whether it appears that way to you or not. This is a supportive Universe, ruled by an amazing intelligence and unconditional love.

Before we were born, we agreed to contracts of karma that must be played out in some way. The way you exchange karmic energy within the Universe is up to you. It's been my experience that whenever you look at your life under a microscope, it can appear cruel and terribly unfair. But when you look at life from the eagle's perspective, from far above, life does have a harmony and an overall balance.

Some things are just painful. Even though we get through tough times, we may hold on to the pain in their wake. This pain becomes part of our foundation, our frame of reference. It's like leaving a window dirty, so that even the sun's light is distorted as it attempts to shine through. Visualization and meditation are stepping-stones to healing. They are in no way intended to replace getting professional advice and help, and by no means am I suggesting that lighting a candle can whisk away all dark thoughts. But it is a start. I believe you have the ability to heal yourself—everyone does. Using rituals and magick to set your intent to face fears, manifest desires, and bring healing works. Try it. I believe in *you*.

Before you cast a spell, you must ask yourself five questions:

**1.** Have you done everything you can on the mundane level? In other words, if you want a new bike or a car, have you investigated which bike or car will best fit your needs, and have you tried to earn money?

**2.** Will it harm anyone? Harm None and do what you will is the number one rule of magick.

**3.** Is it for your highest good? Remember, you only have one frame of reference, one background. The Divine Spirit has access to unlimited ways of seeing how dreams can be met.

**4.** Are you ready to accept the consequences of your spellcasting? If it serves your highest good, your needs will be met, but not always in the package you most desire. When you cast a spell, part of the contract is that you are willing to accept whatever form the Divine chooses to fill your needs.

**5.** Does it go against another's free will? Magick must always respect others' free will to choose. You should never cast a spell that imposes your will upon anothers. Even love spells should be cast upon yourself—to make you more desirable—not cast upon someone else.

Spellwork is part of ritual magick, which generally includes eleven basic elements:

**Welcoming with oil and blessing**

**Centering**

**Grounding and raising a cone of power**

**Drawing a circle of protection**

**Calling in the quarters, guides, and guardians**

**Welcoming God and Goddess**

**Spellwork or spellcasting**

**Enjoying cakes and ale (or juice)**

**Lowering the cone of power**

**Giving thanks and bidding farewell**

**Erasing the circle**

Welcome each participant with oil, incense, or sage smoke. This cleansing, purifying step makes it clear to participants that the time has come to drop the cloak of the mundane, where life happens in an orderly fashion, and welcomes them to the magickal realm of infinite possibilities.

Clear your mind of all thoughts. Breathe deeply and follow your rising and falling breath with your mind's eye. Find the center of your balance. This meditative breath work is called "centering."

Now ground yourself by visualizing tree roots extending from your feet and imagine that your very being can stretch to the fiery heart of Mother Earth. Hook your roots to the Mother's heart center and draw up her silver energy through the many layers of the earth to your own heart center. Hold up your hands and visualize your energy reaching up to a star or the sun. Hook up to the masculine energy of the golden light and watch it circle down to you. Send that energy in a circle clockwise if you are in a group (this is the process of raising a cone of power).

Now the time has come to draw a magickal circle. This circle is intended to separate you from the distractions and restrictions of the mundane world, also known as the third dimension. With your pointer finger or an athame (ritual knife), draw a circle around you in a clockwise direction. You can imagine your circle being defined by a colored light or any other delineation. Say

> *I draw this circle as a boundary between*
> *the world of Spirit and the world of physical,*
> *so that magick may come to the earth plane.*

Next, ask for protection and guidance from the four directions, also called Watchtowers, quadrants, or guardians. You can welcome the four directions by calling upon the corresponding elements, magickal tool, archangels, animals, or elemental beings. As you practice magick, I encourage you to add your own associations with the four directions; however, here are some examples of how they usually match up:

| East | ~ | South | ~ | West | ~ | North |
|------|---|-------|---|------|---|-------|
| Air | ~ | Fire | ~ | Water | ~ | Earth |

Bell ~ Candle ~ Cauldron ~ Salt

Raphael ~ Michael ~ Gabriel ~ Uriel

Eagle ~ Dragon ~ Dolphin ~ Stag

Butterfly ~ Lizard ~ Salmon ~ Spider

Hummingbird ~ Horse ~ Otter . ~ Turtle

Sylph ~ Salamander ~ Undine ~ Faery/Gnome

Beginnings ~ Energy ~ Emotions ~ Grounding

Inspiration ~ Sensuality ~ Nurturing ~ Ancestors

Maiden ~ Temptress/ ~ Mother ~ Crone
Enchantress

You can use music, singing, lighting candles, or whatever feels right to you to call up the energy from the four sacred directions. Working in harmony with them creates magick. The fifth sacred thing is Spirit or love. These five holy things interconnected within the circle of life makes the sign of the pentacle.

As you call upon the God and Goddess in the next step, you are essentially calling upon the Divine Male and Female within yourself to be present. This is the Divine Spirit—the spark of light and life that exists within every human being. When you seek that divine light in yourself and others, true miracles happen. Welcome the Goddess and God. Offer a little drink or a toast to the Goddess and a bit of bread, seed, or corn to the God. Drink and eat as well.

Now is the time for actual spellcasting. Set your intention, ask for your greatest desire, or release something that no longer serves your highest good. You can write it down, bury it, burn it, flush it, freeze it, or place it on your altar. You can tie knots in a cord;

three or nine knots is the usual number. Do what feels right and powerful for you. You can speak your intention or wish out loud, paint, dance, play music, or use any form of expression that works for you.

Now imagine the energy of the cone of power unhooking, spiraling down from the star, and sprinkling stardust upon you. As you visualize the cord or roots that locked you into Mother Earth's heart dissolving, take whatever love and energy you need. This is similar to how a newborn sucks up the last nutrients from the umbilical cord.

Give thanks to the God and Goddess and the four elements for their assistance. Say something like this:

> Stay if you will, go if you must.
> Hail and farewell. Blessed be.

With your pointer finger or an athame, erase the circle around you in a counterclockwise direction. Say

> I now erase the circle and return the space to the human world.
> The circle is now open yet remains unbroken.
> Merry meet. Merry part. Merry meet again.

Casting a circle before doing each spell increases your ability to draw upon your power and do magick. In most cases, it is a necessary step to learning how to build energy. I want to say always, but nothing is ever that absolute. Magickal tools are temporary playthings. All you really need is a focused mind and a pure heart. The goal is to one day be able to focus your energy so precisely and powerfully that you simplify your circle, merely saying, "Powers above, powers below, powers to the right of me, to the left of me, behind me, and in front of me, I call upon you now." And boom, the Divine and your host of angels and guides are ready to help. It's something to work toward.

Before performing any of the rituals described in the rest of the chapter, read through the description thoroughly. You may need to make advance preparations to get certain items to have on hand for the ritual.

# Spells

## ACCEPT YOURSELF

Accepting whatever has happened or is happening is the first step toward happiness. When something terrible happens, if we run from it and don't look at it or accept that it happened, we imprison a part of ourselves in that horrible incident. This is called "disassociation" or "fragmentation." This imprisoned part of us escapes to a place where it wanders in limbo until we choose to clear and heal. In other words, until we consciously choose to acknowledge and accept the reality of the events that caused the fragmented parts of ourselves to leave, they won't be coming home anytime soon.

Most healing comes with subtle changes. Even the smallest shifts in perception can make all the difference in the world. You *can* find that silver lining in every horribly wonderful thing that happens to you. By finding one beautiful lesson in your situation, you can begin to shift your perception and free yourself from the perceived prison you've been keeping yourself in. You are both prisoner and warden. Understand, accept, and love this life and its earthly boundaries, its realms of limitations. You are the Goddess, and an eternal light. You can be dimmed but never snuffed out. Have faith that you are supported to shine as the light that you came to be.

Accepting yourself means that you take a very clear and honest look at who you are. It begins with an internal search to clear away baggage—stale ideas, negative beliefs, and self-deprecating thoughts. It is a spiraling journey into the depths of your soul to the quietness of your power. From this space of knowing both your unique strengths and your damaging patterns of behavior and self-talk, acceptance can blossom. Without an overblown ego or being a cringing wallflower, look into the mirror and just accept what you see without judgment. This acceptance leads to self-love and a kind of luminosity that emanates like a beam of light, attracting love of equal bliss and beauty. That love can come anywhere—from a boy, a girl, friends, parents, siblings, pets, anyone.

Perform this ritual on an auspicious evening, perhaps a full or new moon or a Friday (the day devoted to Freya, Venus, and Aphrodite, all goddesses of love). Anoint four (representing the four faces of the Goddess, as well as stability) pink or white candles with an essential oil that appeals to you. Flowers such as rose, lavender, jasmine, or chamomile are often used in love spells, so any of these would work wonderfully. Oils can be purchased either online or at natural foods markets.

Light the candles. Take ten deep breaths, watching the flames flicker. Feel your womb, the center of your feminine essence. Imagine a cord from your womb dropping into the depths of Mother Earth. Know you are fully supported on this journey. Imagine you are in a forest glen. You see an opening in a tree and are guided to walk through the tree. As you pass through, you discover a spiral staircase. Imagine yourself walking down this staircase. At each turn you have the opportunity to shed a facet of your being that no longer serves you. This can be self-criticism, a judgmental attitude, self-destructive behaviors, or anything that hurts. Imagine there is a beautiful goddess at three different bends. Give each goddess a gift of your unwanted aspects.

Continue down this spiral until you reach the bottom, where there's a pool. Immerse yourself in the luxuriant, fragrant-smelling, warm pool. Know that this vulnerability, the nakedness of your soul without negative attachments, is who you truly are. Hold this image as long as you need. When you are ready, emerge from the pool and walk up the spiral staircase. At each turn where you gave up an unwanted aspect, there stands the same goddess. She has transformed your unwanted gift, offering you a gift of strength, courage, and beauty. The transformation may be into butterflies, birds, colors, or whatever seems right to you. Recognize your talents. She holds a mirror to all the aspects you like and admire in yourself. Your "defects" have been turned into positive attributes. Continue walking up the spiral staircase. Emerge into the forest bedecked as the Maiden Goddess of Love, Aphrodite, ready for enchanted love.

Take ten deep breaths and open your eyes. Draw a bath. Mix together 2 tablespoons kosher salt, 1 tablespoon Epsom salts, 1 tablespoon baking soda, and 10 drops of essential oil. Stir the blend in a clockwise direction, drawing upon the image of yourself as a goddess of love. Pour the mixture into your bath. Immerse yourself in the "pool." Take a handful of rose petals and sprinkle them over yourself. Repeat the phrase "I am love" several times. When you are ready, emerge. Look into the flames once more. Call out to your love. Know that you are radiating like the light of the candles. Douse the flames, or let the candles burn down if that is your choosing.

Remember, maintaining love is an ongoing process. This ritual will give you a jump start to the new you. But to keep the essence of the magick alive, light a pink or white candle, anointed with your essential oil, every month or at the turn of each season, whatever fits your schedule.

Record how the ritual worked for you, how you felt doing it, and any changes or adaptations you made. Remember that the ritual may take days or weeks to manifest.

# SEEKING COURAGE

Courage comes from being true to yourself. It is achieved when the only person whose opinion makes a difference to you is you. It's a matter of releasing your desire to control how others perceive you and focusing primarily on what you think of yourself.

There is a pattern to all breakthroughs in life: the greatest, most enlightened moments of success and happiness are often proceeded by bleak, muddled moments of despair. These are times when you must hold on and steady yourself. Try not to lash out at others and make them feel as miserable as you do. Do your best to not wallow too long in self-pity or project the blame onto others. Instead, realize this moment can be a source of great pride if you act with courage and grace.

Use the elements to create whatever magick you need for this ritual. If the moon is waning, think about releasing fear's hold on you. If the moon is waxing, focus on increasing your courage. The same works for colors and scents. If you are attracted to dark colors or heavy scents, you need to imagine banishing. If you're drawn to lighter colors or smells, imagine the light of confidence and your guiding angels. Magick is created by your intentions, so the form your rituals take has to make sense to you. Take the guidelines I suggest and, if you choose, alter them to create your own spell for courage. Follow your instincts.

On a Tuesday at dusk, stand tall as a tree. Tuesday is the day of Mars, the deity you will be invoking, and dusk is the time of the day when the world of night and the world of day meet and all things seem possible in the space between them. (Feel free to choose other days or times.) Take several deep breaths. Stretch your roots deep into the soil and reach for the sun with your branches. Imagine that you are in a sacred grove of trees where the wind doesn't blow and nothing moves unless it is your will. The entire grove is quiet and cannot be disturbed by any outside influence.

Face the east and ask that the guardians of the element of air come to your aid. Call upon your favorite flying creature. Face the south and ask that the guardians of the element of fire come to your aid. Call upon your favorite animal connected with flames or great will and determination. Face the west and ask that the guardians of the element of water come to your aid. Call upon your favorite animal that swims in the sea. Face the north and ask that the guardians of the element of earth come to your aid. Call upon your favorite animal that roams the earth. You can even choose mythical animals.

Now draw on the energy of the Tree of Life to feed you light so you can call upon the strength and the Divine within yourself. Light a red candle. Place red stones, such as garnets, rubies, or even a rock painted red, around the candle in a circle. Say

*As above, so below.*
*I call upon this wisdom to know.*
*For every vortex there is an apex.*
*In the center of the energies I stand,*
*Ready for courage close at hand.*
*Roots reach deep into Mother Earth.*
*I am stable and strong without another.*
*I stretch to the protection of Father Sky.*
*Empowered by a love that will never die,*

*I call upon Mars, whose power shall start*
*A bright fire of courage that feeds my heart.*

Stand perfectly still with the courage glowing bright in your heart. Know that you are perfectly safe and supported in life. Sit with the candle burning as long as you can. Then, beginning in the north, say good-bye and thank you to each of the four directions, moving in a counterclockwise direction.

Remember there are all kinds of courage—big kinds that take your breath away and little, everyday kinds. And most important, remember that courage is a gift to yourself and to the world. Record how the spell worked for you, how you felt doing the ritual, and any changes or adaptations you made. Remember that the spell may take days or weeks to manifest.

_____

_____

_____

_____

_____

# RECEIVE YOUR POWER

If you've never considered it, you would be amazed to discover how powerful the victim is. The victim receives an immense amount of attention and assistance. Bad things do happen, but you can take charge of your life and soar to great heights without using pity or fluttering eyelashes to get your way.

So let's say something happened that made you feel small and attacked. We often judge a situation and ourselves by labeling an event as "good" or "bad," or thinking "us" versus "them." But there are no absolutes in any situation. There is always a little light in the dark and a little victim in the victor. You must let go of the belief that you are separate from the one who caused you pain. Perhaps you even blame yourself, isolating and shaming a part of yourself.

We are all bound together, connected to Spirit in the tapestry that has been woven not only around us and through us, but through Mother Earth as well. We cannot fully separate from pieces of ourselves or from the one we perceive as the victor. There is a little victor in the victim, especially if you gain anything from your pain. You are here in this world by choice, and you have to meet life on its terms. In order to remember yourself and regain strength and confidence in yourself, you must open Pandora's box and call forth the memory that made you feel like a victim. That which is not named cannot be commanded at will. Energy that is not faced continues to grow and thrive on the food of hate, guilt, shame, and victimhood.

Now take a shower using a loofah, washcloth, or body scrub. Or use the Goddess Sugar Scrub recipe found on page 176. Ask the element of water to cleanse and purify your body. Ask the earth element to release what no longer serves your highest good. See yourself exfoliating thoughts of failure, fear, ridicule, shame, or anything else that haunts you. Watch the negativity spiral down the drain.

Once out of the shower, pamper yourself with a favorite powder, lotion, oil, or perfume. A few recipes for making your own are found in the Potions Lessons (page 157). Smudge yourself and your room (or your house, if you can) with a sage smoke, or use incense if that's easier to access. Visualize the smoke clearing your aura and the room of unwanted energy and sealing it with the protection of love and light.

Write what you want to release on a piece of paper. Place your paper in a fireproof container. Burn it and watch the smoke and flames. Ask the element of air to send your thoughts to Spirit and ask the element of fire to help transform your fears into love, support, success, and peace (or use whatever words seem right for you).

Gather items that represent the desires of your heart. And know completely that it's okay to ask for all that you want. Place the items on an altar. Use stones, leaves, seashells, or anything you wish to mark out a spiral path with your altar at the center. The spiral represents the circular nature of life. Even our lessons seem to happen on a spiral path where we repeatedly visit similar issues at ascending levels of understanding.

Have a container of bubbles, the kind you had as a kid, with a mini wand. Place a broom at the beginning of the path. Step on the broom with your left foot. Release the day, your fears, and as many thoughts as possible. Step over the broom and spin clockwise. Walk the spiral blowing bubble of lightness. Walk the spiral imagining yourself as free to expand as the limitless Universe. Know that your moods and each stage of your life live and then die to make room for new experiences.

Visit your altar. Touch your symbols. Know that all these symbols represent the new state of being you are moving toward. Claim it. Choose to create a life of love and light. You do not need a ballast or anchor to keep you grounded. Blow your bubbles and continue to convey your wishes to Spirit as you walk back out of the spiral.

When it's safe to do so, gather the ashes and feed them to a favorite plant. Roses particularly like ashes. My rose bush nearly doubled in size when I burned my book *The Teen Spell Book* in this ritual. You see, I had reviewed my teen diaries to write the spells, and I used visualizations to see the pain of those years from a new perspective. This created space for a profound healing to take place. Two years after its publication, I was ready to release the pain of the past. The time came to let it all go and allow, through death, a rebirth (perhaps even the birth of this book) of a phoenix will occur. What will you birth by releasing your fears?

Record how this ritual worked for you, how you felt doing it, and any changes or adaptations you made. Remember that the ritual may take days or weeks to manifest.

# WORRY BOX

Let's say you have two days until the big dance, you hate your dress, your date has stopped talking to you, and you don't have enough money to pay for dinner. Or maybe the big game, big test, big whatever is coming and you don't feel ready. It's time for the worry box.

Get a plain box from a craft store. Light a blue candle for the limitless possibility of the sky. Set a lighthearted mood with music or in whatever way feels right to you. Decorate your box with shells, crystals, paints, or symbols of change and transformation. Paint the inside black or fill the box with dark material to represent the womb of all possibilities.

Write down all the horrible things that could happen if everything went wrong, or record all the ways it could go. Let your mind go wild. Shake out all the possible roads your life could take. What keeps you from risking and trusting all will be well? Perhaps you'll be drawn to painting pictures or clipping magazine images. If you are a wordsmith and prefer writing, write down a deeply significant phrase or word and brainstorm about that phrase or word. Fears hide like an itch. They've constructed an ego, an identity and way of being, that doesn't want to die. So you want to make sure you look for all the possible innuendos affecting you and causing you fear. Now it's time to let it all go. Fold the paper away from you and place it in the box. Close the box and say

> I now give to the Goddess this problem of mine.
> I hand over worries and fears to the Divine.

*I trust things will work out just as they should.*
*I know I will be blessed and it's all good.*
*By My Will so Mote It Be!*
*This I make true*
*Three times three times three.*

Douse the blue candle and do your best to not think about your problem. Worrying is like paying interest on a debt you may never owe. What we imagine is usually much worse than reality. Worrying blocks miracles from coming into your life. When you're focused on the worst-case scenario, amazing wonderful things can't even enter the realm of possibility for you. Clear your mind of all the things that could happen, for good or for ill, and try to not think about it for a while. Then the angels can provide a new solution that will be better than anything you could have conceived alone.

After several weeks have passed, open the box and see how the reality compares to your fears. Keep a record of how things work out when you get out of the way and allow the Divine to work miracles in your life. You can reuse your worry box any time worries or fears bog you down.

THE ENCHANTED DIARY

# DRAMA QUEEN

Magick occurs when we change our perspective or view of any situation. There are now wonderful movies and TV programs about magick that show witches can be good. Hopefully they also convey that witches and magickal practitioners are real people with real problems. The flip side of all the Hollywood attention is that movie magick uses sleight of hand to create an illusionary world and, with it, the expectation that if you can't levitate, you aren't a good little witch. I know of no witch or Wiccan who can wrinkle her nose and disappear, cause a feather to rise in the air, or make a spoon stir her coffee. Not that we haven't tried, mind you! But, it won't work. Magick isn't performed for tricks. Magick is practiced to create a connection to All That Is.

Whenever I need to feel the presence of my grandmother, who died one month before I was born, I ask the wind to bring her to me. The only smell I can relate to her is the scent of old photographs—a fragrance I am gifted with in the oddest of locations when my need is most strong. Others in the Craft call upon deities in times of need, and some pretty cool things happen. But very rarely do magickal folk ask elements or deities to perform tricks for pleasure or amusement. That would be a violation of the trust established between human beings and the powers unseen. Real magick doesn't involve flying on broomsticks or casting spells or hexes on other people, and bright sparks don't flash out of our wands.

What does occur is astral flying, which is a delightful process of sending one's energy, awareness, or presence to another time

**Rituals and Spells**

or location. Spells are visualizations, affirmations, and declarations to the Universe. I personally don't believe hexing is possible unless you grant permission for another's energy to influence you. The sparks that do shoot out of our wands are invisible threads of light energy. Some people, such as clairvoyants, can see this light, and with practice, most people can feel it. Think about how you feel when someone points at you and speaks harshly. Can you feel it? Will you accept the hex?

You cannot become a witch or perform magick for the sake of special effects. Special effects only create drama—not true magick. Light a white candle to represent possibilities and receptivity. Focus on the flame and concentrate. Remember and reflect on times you used drama to create an illusion of power. Hold onto a quartz crystal and send all those experiences into the crystal to be cleansed and transformed.

Douse the flame. Light a yellow candle for mental clarity and another candle of a color that represents power to you (this could be yellow like the solar plexus chakra, in which case you only need the one candle). Have at hand a small bowl of sand. Think of a time when you centered yourself and truly called up your full potential and power. Trace images of power, such as a horse, mountain, or other symbol, in the sand and say

*Within me is the wisdom and strength of the ages.*
*No longer will my power be confined by cages*
*Of tricks, sparks, and drama used only to impress.*
*My power is true, strong, and rising, Goddess bless.*
*This I make true, three times three times three.*

Write about what you've learned and how these two different experiences of drama and true power made you feel. Can you see how drama creates chaotic, frenetic energy, whereas centering yourself may not be as crazy, but the result is usually better?

_____

_____

_____

_____

_____

_____

_____

_____

_____

_____

_____

_____

_____

_____

_____

_____

_____

_____

_____

_____

_____

_____

_____

# RAISE YOUR VIBRATION

Yin and yang offer a physical example of balance and a way to gain perspective. Yin is the female energy, personified by rest and inner contemplation. Yang is the male energy, personified by action and movement. The yin yang symbol shows a half-black, half-white circle divided by a curving line, with a small black circle within the white space and a small white circle within the black space. This aspect of the symbol conveys the idea that peace is achieved when there is a little rest within the action and a little female within the male and, conversely, a little action within the rest and a little male within the female.

Working with the yin yang symbol is practice in dissolving lines of separation between "bad" and "good." Remember, there are no hard-and-fast lines within the yin yang symbol. There is no judgment that one is better than the other, because each exists within the other. Interdependent, they work together in harmony.

On the dark side of the symbol and the small black circle below, glue or paint images that represent yin energy to you. On the light side of the symbol and the small white circle, glue or paint images that represent yang energy to you.

As you work, look for how opposites can complement each other to create a balanced world. Allow any rigidity in your judgments or belief system to become fuzzy. Allow for new possibilities and ways of seeing things. Seeing how the two polar opposites work together can help you see the victim in the victor or the silver lining within a dark cloud.

Then look for images that represent total polar opposites. One end is your heaven and the other is your hell. In between is where you live. Now, as with an accordion, bring the two opposites closer together. See how night holds a little energy of day in the light of the moon and stars and how day holds a little energy of night within the shadows that are cast. Nothing is so far apart from anything else that they are not connected to the whole.

Record how the collage worked for you.

_____

_____

_____

_____

_____

_____

# GET OFF OF MY CLOUD

Everything is energy: from light to money to health to attitude. Energy is in constant motion and can be transformed or redirected with your intent. When we talk of protection spells or rituals, what we're really discussing is reinforcing your boundaries to ensure that unwanted or negative energy does not interfere with you, enter your aura, or affect your thoughts or heart.

Protection can be as simple as safeguarding yourself against negative self-talk or criticism from others, especially as these relate to your dreams or aspirations. The world is a beautiful place, but it can sometimes be a bit of drag. Dreams help us fly over our mundane existence. You need to protect your dreams and your right to be lighter than air; all is truly possible, for the unlimited being you are. Do not let anyone weigh down your cloud. Keep open to practical advice and follow the nudges of Spirit and trusted loved ones. Allow your dreams to be redirected, and remain open to the opportunities at hand. As long as you get what you want or need, there's no need to be attached to the way it manifests. Remember, when one door closes, another opens. That is always the case.

If you find yourself being influenced by another to let go of a dream, if you can't escape the naysayers, first see if there's any wisdom to their words. If all you sense is a rather black, sticky cloud of muck, then consider why you might be leaking energy and feeding their disbelief in your dream.

Light a brown candle, then list all the reasons things won't work out. You might have heard that it takes more muscles to frown than it does to smile. The same is true for negative energy: it just weighs more than positive energy. Draw the image of an anchor, or twenty-pound leaden blocks, or globs of gross, sticky mud that weigh you down. Fold the paper, turning it away from you. Seal it shut with the wax of the candle. At the top of the paper, write "Get off of my cloud." Burn it in a safe fireproof container. Say

> *I call upon the element of fire*
> *To transform these words of loss so dire,*
> *To help me create the dream I desire.*
> *By My Will so Mote It Be!*
> *This I make true*
> *Three times three times three.*

Douse the brown candle and light a gold candle. Use DREAM vertically in this book to create as many acronyms as you can think of; for example, Dare, Risk, Evolve, Adventure, and Mine. Know that we are nothing without our dreams. Give yourself the gift of flight and play with all possibilities.

Stare into the gold candle and visualize your dream coming true. See it, taste it, smell it, feel it, hear it. The Divine gave you a life to enjoy. Manifest your dreams! Record how the spell worked for you.

_____

_____

_____

_____

_____

_____

# SUBLIME SELFISHNESS

Being selfish isn't usually considered a positive trait. Women, especially, have been taught to place the needs of others first, much to the detriment of the health of our minds, bodies, and spirits. Being sublimely selfish and putting your own needs first can sometimes be the very best thing for you and for those you love.

Your bathroom will become your altar for the evening. Gather several fresh gardenia blossoms, a silver candle, a white candle, a pink candle, your favorite sensual essential oil, a small flask with a cup of carrier oil (such as apricot or jojoba oil), freshly cut fruit, and if you wish, a body lotion made with the same fragrance as your bath oil. You might try the recipes in the Potions Lessons chapter (page 157). When you choose your favorite aroma, think decadent and sensuous—maybe rose, neroli, or ylang-ylang. The important thing is that the scent is pleasing to you and makes you feel beautiful! Add ten drops of your essential oil to the carrier oil. While you do this, concentrate on self-love.

Fill the bathtub with hot water, along with your exquisite fragrance oil, then gently remove the gardenia petals and add them to your bath. Meditate on the gardenia's gifts of confidence, a positive self-image, your Goddess-given sexuality, and great happiness. Make sure your luscious freshly cut fruit is on a pretty dish by your bath, waiting to be enjoyed as you submerge yourself in beauty. Thoughtfully undress yourself. Pay attention to each newly uncovered body part and smile with appreciation at its sensuous beauty. Then light your candles (hopefully you can place them in front of a mirror). Start by lighting the white candle while meditating on its healing properties and how it symbolizes the presence of Spirit. Then light the pink candle as you meditate on loving yourself and your own special uniqueness. Finally, light the silver candle, which represents the Goddess to you and the Goddess within you. Turn out the lights and admire your lovely face in the glow of these magickally charged candles. Really give yourself time to look into the mirror and appreciate the glow within your eyes. Now recite your spell. Say

*Selfishly I steal away to indulge myself in this magickal bath,*

*Knowing that the love and care it gives me will mean wonderful things to all who cross my path.*

*This I make true three times three times three.*

Now step in and enjoy! The key to this ritual is making it very clear to everyone in your household, and to yourself, that you are taking the night off and that they (or work, school, and the like) won't have you until the next day. Once your bath has come to an end don't stop there: rub a nice lotion with the same fragrance as your bath into your damp skin, then wrap yourself in a cozy terry cloth robe. Now go and enjoy a good book or just turn in for a restful night of sleep. Be selfish. It's okay. Remember, you are a goddess and deserve to be pampered and spoiled. Blessed be!

Record how the spell worked for you, how you felt doing the ritual, and any changes or adaptations you made. Remember that it may take days or weeks to manifest all the gifts of a newfound self-image.

# INCREASE YOUR BLISS TOLERANCE

For some, increasing your bliss tolerance sounds a bit strange or funky. What this means is feeling comfortable being happy and free of worry or fear. You don't need to complain about your parents, your body, or your grades or say that nobody understands you to be cool. It doesn't mean you're stuck up if you accept things as they are and you're happy. I remember a time during my senior year of high school when a bunch of girls and I stood in front of the mirrors in the bathroom. Everyone was complaining about how big their butt was, a zit on their nose, how stringy their hair looked, whatever. And for the first time, I looked in the mirror and didn't see any of those things. I was truly okay with my reflection. I wasn't perfect like a model, but that didn't matter. It was a good feeling, except that I felt conceited because I did not have anything to fret about. Who puts those kinds of thoughts in our head anyway?

It's time to get cozy with feeling good about life, about your life in particular, and about yourself. Just because there are ways you might improve upon your life doesn't need to stop you from finding peace and bliss today. Since the path to bliss is actually quite simple, this ritual will reflect the same effortless qualities.

Begin by setting aside some time when you won't be distracted. Follow your breath; ride it like a wave. Allow thoughts to come and go, but don't dwell on anything for too long. Now become aware of your surroundings through your five senses. How does the room smell? What do you see? Touch things around you. Listen for familiar and unfamiliar sounds. Taste something simple, like a piece of gum, a sip of juice, or a bite of an apple. Find comfort in the familiarity of your surroundings.

Now put all your attention on your heart center. Feel your breath enter your heart. Notice how you feel. Don't judge; just be aware and accept. Now think about all the things you have to be grateful for. Create a list if that feels right to you. Acknowledging what is going right in your life will attract more of the same, so take a moment to be truly thankful. Light a rainbow-colored candle or small candles of each color of the rainbow. Concentrate on each color in turn, imagining how you can express your gratitude through what each of the colors represents to you. Look up the color meanings on page 27 or just use the qualities that each color represents to you. Visualize yourself pushing against the borders of discontent, sadness, or apathy to create a space for bliss and happiness to enter. In your mind's eye, see a rainbow of happiness and rewards pouring into your life. See yourself holding a cup and watch as the gifts fill then spill out of the cup. Say

*I now create a space to fill with*
*Bliss and happiness through my will.*
*Rewards and joys will enter in*
*As I find light shining within.*
*By My Will so Mote It Be!*
*Three times three times three.*

Remember to share your wealth and happiness whenever you can—your cup is overfilled, why not give a little? Gratitude and sharing are the keys to inner happiness. Record how the ritual worked for you, how you felt doing it, and any changes or adap-

THE ENCHANTED DIARY

tations you made. Remember that the spell may take days or weeks to bring about a feeling of bliss.

# POTIONS LESSONS

e live in two worlds—the visible and the invisible. The invisible thoughts, feelings, intents, and emotions are the driving force, absolutely essential to the manifestation of the visible. You can create anything you can imagine. Everything you make, whether things or relationships, first begins as a thought. These thoughts or intents go into your creations, like any other ingredient. In fact, your intent is the most powerful ingredient there is. Working with magick requires you to believe in the power of the unseen. If you're having trouble with this concept, consider this: we can't see love and sadness, but we feel them nonetheless.

Creating potions with essential oils is an excellent way to begin creating a life of your choosing. As you mix these simple potions, concentrate on an intent. Your personal imprint and intent will go into the potion and create the true magick.

Following is a list of common essential oils, along with the oils' magickal and healing properties. When you buy essential oils, be sure to get oils that are 100 percent essential oil. Some oils are diluted with a base oil or are chemically created in a lab (perfume oils). The best place to get oils is either at a natural foods store or online, for example, at Mountain Rose Herbs (www.mountain-roseherbs.com) or Auracacia (www.frontiercoop.com), are excellent resources.

The main reason you want to get organic 100 percent pure oils is because these oils are distilled from the actual plant, not created in a beaker. They are pulsating with the life force of the plant. This magickal and healing power comes from Mother Earth. How can you possibly ask an oil to create relaxation if it's disconnected from the Source? When you work with herbs and oils, you are attempting to invoke the powers of Mother Earth, the same living, breathing energy within you that knows how to knit bones or calm an angry mind.

Play with the oils. Try mixing them together. You'll find that some oils smell great separately, but horrible together. The scent of oils is divided into three parts: the top note, a scent you smell first, but eventually floats away; the middle note, a scent that comes after the top note, stays awhile, then dissipates; and the base note, a scent that lingers the longest. The base note will give staying power to the lighter notes as well. Citrus oils, like bergamot, grapefruit, and lemon, are considered top notes. Essential oils made from flowers (chamomile and geranium) are usually middle notes, with the exception of ylang ylang, which is a base note. Essential oils made from the bark or root, such as cinnamon, myrrh, or sandalwood, are base notes.

# ESSENTIAL OILS

### Benzoin
  acne, anxiety, loneliness, peace, purification, scars

### Bergamot
  (Citrus aurantium var. bergamia) acne, balance, immune
  booster, mood swings, prosperity, protection (especially
  against sexual harassment), stress

### Cedarwood, Atlas
  (Cedrus atlantica) acne, anger, anxiety, nervousness

### Chamomile, Roman
  (Anthemis nobilis) acne, anger, anxiety, cold sores,
  cramps, depression, headache, insomnia, stomachache,
  yeast infections

### Cinnamon
  (Cinnamomum zeylanicum) anxiety, anorexia, cramps,
  fevers, illumination, meditation, menses regulation,
  protection, sensuality, yeast infections

### Eucalyptus
  (Eucalyptus globules) breathing problems, bruises,
  concentration, depression, headache, healing,
  purification, sore muscles, yeast infections

### Frankincense

(Boswellia sacra) anointing, blessings, clairvoyance, concentration, manifestation, prosperity, protection, purification

### Geranium

(Pelargonium graveolens) acne, anointing, courage, healing, love, protection

### Ginger

(Zingiber officinale) anorexia, bruises, cramps, headache, healing, motion sickness, sensuality

### Jasmine

(Jasminum officinale) anointing, attracting love, confidence, meditation, memory, mysteries, prophetic dreams, sunburn

### Lavender

(Lavandula officinalis) acne, anorexia, headache, healing, insomnia, purification, scars, stress, sunburn

### Neroli

(Citrus aurantium var. amara) acne, anger, anorexia, anxiety, cramps, depression, fear, headache, insomnia, peace, scars, sensuality, yeast infections

## Patchouli

(Pogostemon cablin or Pogostemon patchouli) acne, depression, love, peace, prosperity, protection, scars, sensuality

## Peppermint

(Mentha piperita) acne, bruises, creating change, relaxation

## Rose attar

*(aka Rose otto)* (Rosa damascena) anger, clairvoyance, compassion, concentration, guilt, fluid retention, headache, insomnia, peace, stress, sunburn

## Rosemary

(Rosmarinus officinalis) abundance, acne, anorexia, fluid retention, grounding, headache, memory, protection, purification

## Sandalwood

(Santalum album) acne, anointing, depression, healing, insomnia, intuition, protection, stress

## Vetiver

(Vetiveria zizanoides) acne, anxiety, bruises, depression, insomnia, scars, stress

# Perfectly You Perfume

*¹/₂ ounce unscented carrier oil, such as jojoba, almond, or ven pure olive oil*

*5 to 7 drops of your favorite essential oil or a blend of oils*

Have you noticed how the same perfume smells different on different people? Or that one perfume can even smell different on you depending upon your mood? We each have a personal scent, something as individual and unique as our fingerprints. Our chemical makeup creates this scent, so that when we are on our moon (period or menses) or experience different emotions, we may even smell a bit different.

Westerners spend tons of money trying to cover up their scent. What are we trying to hide? I say, alchemize it. Try making a perfume that enhances your personal scent. When you create a perfume, you don't want to make it overwhelming. Something subtle to draw people to you without assaulting them with your intensity. Create a perfume for a mood, say sensuality, or for a time of the year, or to invoke confidence or courage. It's up to you.

There are lots of ways to create perfume. Try setting out your essential oils in front of you. Close your eyes and pass your hand through the air above the oils. Feel for a magnetic pull toward an oil. Pour the carrier oil into your perfume bottle, then add the essential oil one drop at a time. See what healing or magickal properties the oil carries. Write about why you think your intuition chose this oil. You can also use the list of the essential oils at the beginning of this chapter to create an oil that matches a need you want fulfilled. Or you can create a perfume just because you like the way it smells.

---

Record your favorite blends and write about what happened when you wore them.

# Beautifying Bath Salts

*¹/₃ cup Dead Sea salt*

*¹/₃ cup baking soda*

*¹/₃ cup Epsom salts*

*5 to 7 drops of essential oil*

Taking a salt bath is an excellent way to ground yourself. Salt represents the earth element and can help you get in touch with your body and your life. Sometimes we can get too wrapped up in our emotions. You may have heard the phrases "She's a slave to her emotions" or "You need to get control of your emotions." Or maybe your life feels too hectic or your mind is spinning away without you: "She's way too much in her head."

If ever you feel as though your emotions have the best of you or you're caught in analysis paralysis, don't try to rein yourself in, as if you were a wild horse in need of taming. Try a little indulgence and compassion instead. Call on the powers of the earth with salt and use calming waters to bring you to centeredness. When you're in balance, your mind, body, and emotions work in harmony. In this recipe, use an essential oil that makes you feel at peace with yourself and the world. Enjoy!

Mix the sea salt, baking soda, and Epsom salts together. Focus on your intent, whether that is relaxing, purification, protection, or some other need. Add the essential oil 2 drops at a time until the blend smells just right. You can also add food coloring or natural plant dyes for a little color. This recipe makes 1 cup. Use about $^1/_2$ cup per bath. Store the bath salts in an airtight container and use them within a year.

---

You can have fun creating labels or decorating the jar. Try stick-on crystals or paint the jar, perhaps using magickal designs. Or cut a square piece of fabric, glue it on the jar's rim, and tie it off with a piece of hemp or raffia cord. These bath salts make great gifts, too.

---

Try making blends at different phases of the moon. Or take a bath with the same blend at different phases of the moon. Take notice of how the moon and different blends affect you. Record your favorite recipes and what thoughts and intents you infused into them.

# Faery Dust

*¹/₃ cup white kaolin clay*

*¹/₃ cup arrowroot powder*

*¹/₃ cup cornstarch*

*¹/₂ teaspoon powdered mica*

*10 drops of your favorite essential oil or a blend of oils*

Faeries are wild, with creative and destructive sides. They appreciate that both aspects are essential to life. Humans, on the other hand, tend to believe that destruction is evil, but that's a man-made idea. Why would it be evil that compost makes fresh grass or that the fruits that fall from the tree feed the roots themselves? Let us all try to be more comfortable with the ways of nature. Life changes—that's something you can count on. It's only our fear of the unknown that causes us to want to label change as evil.

Faeries are particularly known for using shimmer and twinkle in their magick. They tempt and tease their human playmates until we learn to let go a little and have some lighthearted fun. Their playful, mischievous nature is quite similar to the unfettered or carefree qualities of the Enchantress. Using this body powder will empower you with Goddess sheen without having to use chemicals.

Combine the clay, arrowroot, cornstarch, and mica ingredients in a blender. Then add the essential oil and blend again. Put the powder into a salt shaker, or try the glass jars more commonly used for red pepper flakes and Parmesan cheese at Italian restaurants and pizza joints (you can get jars at grocery stores and warehouse stores like Costco). This Faery dust potion will make about one cup.

---

Record the thoughts and intents you infused into this potion.

_____

_____

_____

_____

_____

_____

_____

_____

_____

# Razor Burn Salve

*¹/₃ cup dried comfrey leaves*

*1¹/₂ cups water*

*¹/₄ cup beeswax*

*20 drops of tea tree essential oil*

This salve is perfect for little nicks and wounds as well as for immediate relief from razor burn, even on those sensitive areas. Comfrey is known as "knitbone" because it encourages tissues, bones, and ligaments to grow back together. In magick, comfrey is used in protection spells when traveling.

Bring the water to a boil in a saucepan. Turn off the heat, add the comfrey, and cover with a lid. Allow the infusion to sit for 2 hours. Strain the liquid and discard the comfrey. Pour 1 cup of the comfrey infusion into a saucepan over low heat. Shave or cut the beeswax into small chunks and add it to the infusion. Heat until the beeswax is melted, then remove from the heat and add the tea tree oil. Pour the salve into sterilized containers. This recipe makes about 1 cup. Store the salve in a cool, dark place, and use it within a year. Note: Don't use this salve on cuts deeper than ¹/₄ inch; if the wound is bleeding profusely; or when the wound was caused by a splinter, other foreign object, or an animal bite.

Record the thoughts and intents you infused into this potion.

_____

_____

_____

_____

_____

_____

_____

_____

_____

_____

_____

_____

_____

_____

_____

_____

_____

_____

# Sun-Stoked Lotion

$^{1}/_{2}$ ounce beeswax

$^{1}/_{2}$ cup cocoa butter

$^{1}/_{4}$ cup rosehip seed oil

$^{1}/_{4}$ cup macadamia or almond oil

1 teaspoon vitamin E oil

1 cup distilled water

30 drops carrot seed essential oil

10 drops helichrysum essential oil

10 drops myrrh essential oil

10 drops vanilla essential oil

If you love to soak up the rays, as I do, it's a good idea to have a lotion that can help you repair the cells you cooked while laying out. Plus, this lotion smells great and feels so soothing on sunburned skin. This lotion takes concentration and a bit of time. Look over the directions carefully before you start making it. Never leave the lotion unattended while cooking. You may even prefer to prepare this with adult supervision. That will show some responsibility to counterbalance your defiance of the effects of the thinning ozone layer.

Fill a medium-sized saucepan about a third full with water and bring to a boil. Put the beeswax in a heavy glass or cup and place the cup in the saucepan until the beeswax melts. Then add the cocoa butter, rosehip seed oil, macadamia oil, and vitamin E oil. Heat the mixture until the beeswax is completely melted again (it will harden somewhat when you add the other oils). Remove from the heat and allow the mixture to cool for approximately 10 minutes, or until the beeswax begins to harden around the edges of the cup. Pour the distilled water in a blender and place the lid on the blender. Remove the center from the lid and insert a funnel. Turn on the blender on low speed and slowly pour in the beeswax mixture. As the mixture emulsifies (blends together), you may need to turn off the blender and use chopsticks to stir, then continue blending as needed, until most of the water is absorbed. Add the essential oils and turn on the blender on low speed just long enough to mix in the essential oils. Using a spatula, pour the cream into clean jars. Since there are no preservatives, this cream will only keep for six months to a year. This recipe makes $1^1/_2$ cups or 12 ounces. Store in the refrigerator.

Record the thoughts and intents you infused into this potion.

_____

_____

_____

_____

_____

_____

# Pretty Nails Lotion

2 tablespoons pure kukui nut or avocado oil

4 drops of sandalwood essential oil

4 drops of lemon essential oil

4 drops of lavender essential oil

4 drops of tea tree essential oil

4 drops of benzoin essential oil

10 drops of vitamin E oil

This is a really easy potion for beautiful fingers and nails. As you make this recipe, concentrate on the way you'd like your fingers to look. This is a perfect lotion for those gals who like to use their hands when they talk. Also great for toenails!

Combine all the ingredients in a 2-ounce small jar and mix well. Apply two drops to each nail and four drops to each hand and massage in.

Record the thoughts and intents you infused into this potion.

# Kissable Lips

2 tablespoons beeswax

$^1/_2$ cup jojoba oil

1 teaspoon honey

1 teaspoon aloe vera gel

10 drops tea tree essential oil

5 drops peppermint essential oil

Who wouldn't want kissable lips? This little lip salve uses the healing elements of tea tree oil and aloe and the zing of peppermint to ensure you have soft, supple lips. If you're having a difficult time attracting that perfect kissable partner, as you mix the ingredients, stir clockwise, the way the sun appears to move in the northern hemisphere and the pattern of creation. Imagine the feelings that arise from that special first kiss. When you add the aloe vera and tea tree oil, imagine that this relationship or kiss nourishes your soul, like a gentle wave of bliss. As you add the peppermint oil, imagine the electrifying tremor that blazes through you, setting your hair on end. Mmm, good stuff.

In a small saucepan, melt the beeswax over low heat. Stir in the jojoba oil, honey, aloe vera gel, and tea tree oil. Cook until warm, then remove from the heat. Stir rapidly with a whisk until cool, then add the peppermint oil. The recipe makes about $^2/_3$ cup balm. Pour the balm into small containers. Apply it to your lips to help prevent and heal chapping, cracking, or blisters, and to create smooth, kissable lips!

---

Record the thoughts and intents you infused into this potion.

_____

_____

_____

_____

_____

_____

_____

_____

_____

_____

# Goddess Sugar Scrub

*¹/₂ cup organic white sugar*

*¹/₄ cup apricot kernel oil*

*¹/₄ teaspoon citric acid*

*1 teaspoon aloe vera gel*

*1 teaspoon cocoa butter*

*6 drops bergamot or grapefruit essential oil*

Scrubs exfoliate and polish the skin, stimulate cell renewal, and promote velvety soft, smooth skin. I use sugar in this recipe because it contains glycolic acid, one of the natural alpha hydroxy acids that exfoliate the skin. Bergamot and grapefruit oil are used because of their benefits for skin. Make this scrub during a new moon. New moons are a time to let go of bad habits, reflect, and pay attention to your inner guidance. As you mix the ingredients, consider what you can let go of. Visualize yourself as being born anew, fresh and stronger than before.

Mix together the sugar, apricot kernel oil, citric acid, and aloe vera. Gently warm the cocoa butter by placing the container in a bowl of hot water to soften it. Add the cocoa butter to the sugar mixture and combine using a hand mixer on high speed for 3 to 5 minutes.

Add the essential oil. This recipe makes about ¹/₂ cup or 6 ounces.

In the shower, wet your skin, then rub the sugar scrub all over your body. Rinse, but do *not* wash with soap afterward. Be sure to rinse out the tub before the ants come marching in. You can use this scrub up to twice a week.

Record the thoughts and intents you infused into this potion.

_____

_____

_____

_____

_____

_____

_____

_____

_____

# OUR STORIES

This small collection of stories about the Enchantress years was crafted to champion your ability to trust your instincts, empower your will, and find the power that will sustain you. The Goddess is the keeper of this cycle of life. She has four faces: the Maiden, who is light and beginnings; the Temptress or Enchantress, who is creativity and individuality; the Mother, who is fullness and creativity; and the Crone, who is wise and the reaper. Since every woman is a Goddess, each of the archetypes exists in every woman at all times. You come to know the different faces of the Goddess—Maiden, Enchantress, Mother, and Crone—in a deeper way when you're at the stage of life when each fully blossoms.

Life is constantly on the move. The Goddess, the Universe, everything, is constantly evolving, and that can be unnerving. I happen to find life's road easier if someone tells me their story. I find laughter, camaraderie, and courage in sharing with those who have gone before me. Sharing our stories helps us heal each other, and the world. Hopefully, you'll find support and come to know that you're not alone in whatever phase, dark or light, you may be passing through. And you will rise above all perceived problems.

# Mean Girls

I was quite happy in school that year, at least in the beginning. But one girl, Emily, seemed to not be enjoying the year at all. She always wore dark colors that matched her long black hair and dark brown eyes. She was very quiet, only talking when the teacher called on her. During recess she sat in the classroom with her head in her arms, and she never played with or spoke to any other classmates.

I didn't know why Emily never played or talked with anyone, until one day the mystery was solved. It was at my friend Britney's birthday party. We were all playing in the pool. All the girls from our class were there. But wait! Emily wasn't there. I wondered why. Maybe she was busy. But I wanted to know, so I asked, "Where's Emily?"

Everybody stopped talking and they all stared at me. "Emily?" Britney asked, her eyebrows raised. "I don't invite creeps like her to my parties." Soon everybody was remarking about Emily's "stupid" personality, her "stupid" fashion, and anything else they could think of to criticize about her.

I didn't understand why nobody liked her. After all, it was already February, and our class had welcomed all the other new-comers except Emily. But I didn't try to change anything. I was afraid that if I hung out with Emily, all my other friends would turn against me and make fun of me.

I was happy in school, but at home I felt sorry for Emily. Things began getting worse as the year continued. People in our class began shouting horrible remarks at her and "accidentally" did things like trip her or spill drinks on her. She cried a lot and the teachers tried to stop the students, but nothing changed. The girls would plan to hang out and watch movies right in front of Emily and never invited her. I was always invited to these get-togethers, but I felt bad every time I went. More and more, I began making up excuses why I couldn't go.

Finally, I decided I had to do something about this problem instead of waiting around for someone else to solve it. Little by little, I began talking to Emily. At first she ignored me, thinking I was part of the "mean group." But by and by she started talking, and soon we were talking during recess and eating lunch together. All my other friends turned against me and began making fun of me as well as Emily. They excluded me from the after-school activities and didn't talk to me anymore. But I didn't show them I was hurt. And as I struggled, I became stronger. So did Emily. She didn't cry when she was made fun of anymore, and we both had more self-confidence.

In the middle of April, two of my old friends, who used to be in Britney's group, got fed up with Britney's constant complaints and bossiness. They began talking to Emily and me. More and more of the girls began talking to Emily and me. More and more of the girls began talking to Emily. Finally, Britney was left alone and friendless. But before we could all make up with her and filter out the negative feelings, she left the school.

Now Emily had many friends and was never excluded from anything. I had learned not to fear what everyone thought about me if I made a certain choice. My breaking away from the popular group and moving to the unpopular group had led others to discover that as well.

Lisa, 14

Throughout the tempest of the teen years, it's difficult to know who you truly are when the group you hang out with or the music you listen to seems to define who you are. Obviously, you are more than what you identify with. But how do you stand up for yourself and what you believe in when it feels like you'll lose everything if you do? The Mexican revolutionist Emiliano Zapata said, "It's better to die on your feet than live a lifetime on your knees." Write about times when you've stood up to others or stood up for your integrity? How did that make you feel?

# Grandmother's Legacy

1954: I'm seven years old, always under the feet of my *yiayia*'s (Greek for "grandmother"), especially in the kitchen. There is the familiar smell of the sweet blend of ingredients cooking on the stove in a small, long-handled brass pot. Today is different: I've been formally invited to the gathering of women in our family to sit down, drink what comes out of that pot in very small, delicate cups and saucers, and partake in the ritual that follows.

1962: I'm fifteen years old, spending the summer learning how to cook Greek food in the kitchen with YiaYia. I would rather go to the beach with my cousin. I came here to play: the last thing I came up here for was to work. Over breakfast, YiaYia gently reminds me that she is in charge. Resigned to my torture, I wash the breakfast dishes. Afterward, she notices my long face and starts making this funny clucking noise as she hands me the familiar, long-handled brass pot.

She says, "It's time to learn a little Greek magic." For the first time, I notice how tiny and graceful her hands are. "There are two of us, so take two demitasse cups and fill them with water, pour the water out of the cups into the brass pot, and put the pot on the stove."

I wonder to myself, has YiaYia always been so small? "Next, put a teaspoon of sugar per cup in the pot, then put in a generous teaspoon of powdered Greek coffee per cup (you can also use Turkish coffee) and turn on the stove, YiaYia says. "Watch, because when it starts to boil, the coffee floating on the top of the water will crack. When it does, remove the pot from the fire, count to three, then put the pot back on the stove. When it cracks again, take the pot off the stove, count to three, and put the pot back on the stove for third time. As it starts to boil, count to three, throw a kiss at the pot, and take it off the stove." I do as she says and wait for the next instructions. "Now pour into the cups, making sure they both have the same amount of coffee with equal froth on top. The froth is the start of your fortune, and also the hardest to master. The hardest lessons to master are always connected to, and healed by, love, patience, and faith."

December 5, 1986: I'm thirty-nine years old and Christmas is in full swing, but a veil of sadness dampens any holiday cheer. My father is dying. My yiayia calls to me. She is now a stunning, graceful woman of almost ninety. I am a yiayia now, standing in the same kitchen, cooking with the same brass pot. "The coffee is ready," I say. My mood is gray as I sit down in the living room and pass YiaYia her cup. We sip the pleasantly sweet, thick coffee, and as we do, I look into the face of ancient feminine wisdom, eyes sparkling and so full of mirth that I start laughing. Then the ritual begins.

We slowly drink the coffee all the way to the grounds. We swish the cups around three times clockwise and then turn the cups upside down in the saucers, where they sit for at least five minutes. When we turn the cups back up, the grounds have left patterns in the cup. From this we read our fortunes. We have done this for over thirty years, hundreds of times, but never like this. The hair stands on end all over my body. I hear the crash of thunder in my head and my ears ring. Looking into the cup is dizzying.

"What do you see?" comes a voice that sounds suddenly tired, but also excited.

I reply, "I see a veil of the finest, most delicate lace, with a face underneath at rest. I see a seven on one side of the cup, three doves flying up on the opposite side, and only one path out of the top. I see my father's peaceful death in seven days."

Quietly, my YiaYia takes the cup and looks in for what it seems to be a long time. When she looks up she has tears in her eyes, "You are right," she whispers. In that moment our eyes locked. She takes my hands and says, "For many years, I have watched and waited for this time to come. For this power of sight was given to me, and for a while I thought it would die with me. You have proven where this power is to go, so I freely give to you what was freely given to me. Thus it shall go on as it always has."

YiaYia drank coffee for five more years but refused to read the cups. My father died on the seventh day. Today I teach, and I watch, and someday another woman's day will come.

Connie, ∞

Connie, a very much loved Elder High Priestess of the Crimson Dragon Druidic Craft of the Wise Wiccan coven and proud YiaYia of five beautiful children and a plethora of spiritual kids, entered the world of Spirit two days after this manuscript was complete. It was her wish to pass on her information, her wisdom, her legacy. Remember to enjoy the gifts of our grandmothers.

Listen to the wisdom of your grandmother. What have you learned from her? When could you have learned from an elder, but did not? What would you say to that person now?

---------------------------------------------------------------

---------------------------------------------------------------

---------------------------------------------------------------

# True Self

I was becoming someone I didn't want to be. I was becoming the snotty girl—the one that almost everyone dislikes. I was becoming mean, judgmental, and disrespectful. Before I knew it, I had become one of those popular, rich girls whom everyone dislikes but no one will ever stand up to.

I would disinclude people from my "posse" just because I thought they weren't smart enough or if they didn't obey my every command. I would use people and take advantage of them. I started to slack off in school, and in life. I made people think my life was perfect (which it wasn't). I got bad grades and developed an attitude. That's when people started to tell me outright they hated me. One day my best friend told me that nobody liked me.

That summer I was all alone—no one called. I realized what I was doing was wrong and hurtful to the people I cared about. So I decided to change and become a better person. I changed my fashion sense, I got my ears pierced, and I changed the color of my hair. Most important, I changed the way I looked at the world around me: I tried to see things from others' point of view. I tried to figure out how I could help—be the hero maybe. I changed the way I looked at the world around me just so everyone could accept me. I wanted to stay popular but be nice.

When I came back to school in the fall, almost everything about me was different. People could tell that I had changed and that I gave out a different vibe than I had the previous year. Everyone complimented my clothes, my earrings, the color of my hair, but they had yet to see what was really different about me.

THE ENCHANTED DIARY

Over the next week or so, I was doing really well. I was being kind, accepting, and respectful. I would give people things if they needed them and gave advice if they asked for it. I was being exactly the person I thought I wanted to be. But it wasn't at all what I expected.

At the end of only the third week, I realized what I had become: a pushover. I had become too kind. People were starting to push me around. I had become too accepting. I was hanging around people who teased me and treated me poorly. I had become more respectful of others than of myself, placing myself at a lower status than my friends or anybody else. People began to use me and take advantage of me. And through it all, I still didn't get my wish. I still wasn't accepted by anyone. So I proceeded to change myself again, again, and again. No matter how many times I changed my image or personality, I still wasn't accepted by everyone.

A year after my many transformations, I finally found the missing piece to my puzzle. Throughout all this time, I had been changing myself for other people, never for myself. Once I figured this out, I immediately began to think about what I wanted and how I wanted it, which was something I almost never did. I wanted to have respect for myself and be powerful, but not in a way that others would worship me. I wanted people to see me as a friend who knows how to be strong for herself. I changed my fashion sense again, but I kept my ears pierced, I kept my hair color, and I decided I would be kind, accepting, and respectful as long as others were all those things toward me.

The next fall when I went back to school, people could tell not only that I changed, but also that there was a whole new feeling about me, more so than before. It wasn't because of my clothes, earrings, or hair; it was because I was happy with myself, and just by looking at me you could tell that simple but important fact. Now, just because I was happy with myself didn't mean everyone else was. But it did mean that because I was happy with myself, all those other people didn't matter. And all the people who *were* happy with me got in return a very kind, accepting, and respectful friend.

Shevaun, 14

It's much easier to go with the flow in life than to fight the currents. Adaptability has been the key to survival since the dawn of time. Changing yourself isn't always a bad thing, as long as you don't do it for anyone's pleasure but your own. Life isn't about pleasing other people, it's about pleasing yourself.

Write about the changes you have made that you regret and those you are proud of. What changes have made you a stronger person in the end? What sets those apart from other changes you've made?

_____

_____

_____

_____

_____

_____

_____

_____

_____

_____

# INDEX